Something
to
Thank About
from
A to Z

Thanking and praising God for God through Scripture

"It is a good thing to give thanks unto the LORD,
and to sing praises unto thy name, O most High:"
Psalm 92:1

Hertistine Washington

Xulon PRESS

"Be still and know that I am God:
I will be exalted among the heathen,
I will be exalted in the earth." Psalm 46:10

"Make a joyful noise unto the LORD, all ye lands.
Serve the LORD with gladness:
come before his presence with singing.
Know ye that the LORD he is God:
It is he that has made us, and not we ourselves;
we are his people, and the sheep of his pasture.
Enter into his gates with thanksgiving,
and into his courts with praise:
be thankful unto him, and bless his name.
for the LORD is good; his mercy is everlasting;
And his truth endureth to all generation." Psalm 100

"My heart is inditing a good matter:
I speak of the things which I have made touching the king:
my tongue is the pen of a ready writer." Psalm 45:1

"Because I will publish the name of the LORD;
ascribe ye greatness unto our God." Deuteronomy 32:3

DEDICATED

In memory of my dear sister,
Gertrude (Gina) Cooks,
who first spoke this idea to me,

and

Harvest G. Washington, Sr.,
my loving husband
who continues to grow with me
in expressing our lifelong gratitude to
God for God.

To our four crew members
who daily gives me inspiration
to thank God every day.

Tiffany, Harvest, Jr., Rosie, Willie

TABLE OF CONTENTS

Acknowledgements

*F*irst, and foremost I wish to thank God our heavenly Father through our Lord and Savior Jesus Christ, by the power of the Holy Spirit, for placing this desire within my heart. I humbly acknowledge without Him I can do nothing. He alone was my Guide, Energizer, and Inspirer, as I pursued in this endeavor.

I thank God for giving me the privilege to sit under the teaching and preaching of devout and humble men of the gospel. I thank Him for the legacy of my first Pastor in Los Angeles, the late Robert R. Coston, Sr., who taught me how important it is to memorize, meditate, and pray the Scriptures. I also thank God for my current pastor, Pastor George E. Hurtt, for teaching me how to know God better.

- To my dear husband of 40 years, I acknowledge God for your love, patience, and care for me. I thank Him for your loving support and understanding. I appreciate the many tidbits you've shared along this journey.

- To my children, I thank God for your encouragement, hugs, talents, phone calls, and suggestions. I thank God for allowing you to help me with various technological matters—computer niches, getting online, visiting various websites, downloading, etc. This work wouldn't have come about without Him giving you skillful knowledge in a particular field to help your mom.

Something to Thank About from A to Z

- *To our three beautiful grandchildren, Riana, Jordan, and Lil Harvest, 111, I say, thank you, for encouraging me with your smiles and enthusiasm, "Grandma you can do it!"*
- *To my brothers and sisters: Randy, Andrew, Levi, Jean, and Flo, I love and adore you. Thank you for being there for me.*
- *To my loving aunt Easter Holliday, (the matriarch of our family) I thank God for using your life to also express my deep gratitude to God for God, the ultimate Caregiver.*
- *To my church family (The Mt. Sinai Missionary Baptist Church (http.//sinai.church /), I love and adore you. Thank you for your warmth and support.*
- *I further thank and praise God for His grace in surrounding me with dear friends and associates who willingly shared their expertise. I thank Him for connecting me with a close knit writer's support group, The Xulon Press publishing company, and all who shared their expert skill in bringing this writing from pen to paper; from script to book; from book to your hands; from your hands to your heart; from your heart to others; from others to the praise and glory of God our Heavenly Father.*
- *Last, but not least, I thank God for the life and legacy of my dear sister, Gertrude (Gina) Cooks, who first spoke this idea to me to write a book. I thank God for allowing me to glorify Him in keeping that promise.*

Introduction

In 2005, I was asked to write a book about sisters from my late and loving sister, Gina. It was to be a book expressing gratitude for the love and care shared between sisters during her struggle with breast cancer. At that time, writing a book was not a priority. I just wanted my sister to be healed. Although she has made her transition from earth to eternity, she was healed in many ways, both physically and spiritually. After making her transition, I still didn't have a desire to write a book. I had only a constant nudging in that direction. But now, thanks be to God for placing that desire in my heart.

I had no idea my journaling would be a prelude to a book. Although this book is not directly about sisters, I can certainly conclude every sister, brother, father, mother, and everyone will benefit greatly. During my sister's struggle, I saw that God was not absent, but a very present help in her time of need. As He was to her, so is He to us, a very Present Helper. In lieu of that, this book will contain expressions of deep gratitude to God for God for His love and care to everyone as conveyed through Scripture, along with my personal affirmations of Him.

I spent many years Scripture journaling on the attributes of God as revealed by reading and meditating in His Word, my life experiences, and His teaching. This led me to a deeper appreciation to Him and for Him. I praise God for blessing me to compile my writing in putting pen to paper. I can definitely say thank God for God: my Energizer, Timer, and Inspirer. In a nut shell, this book is about using God's Word to say 'Thank you' to Him and for Him from A to Z.

There are many names, titles, and attributes of God found in His Holy Word. God is so big we can never name them all. God excels beyond what our finite minds can hold. Let's be clear, no one can find out God; He's all-encompassing. Like many of you, I gladly thank God for many things: life, liberty, love, health, family, friends, safety, shelter, food, clothing, etc. For the Scripture says, "Giving thanks always for all things unto God and the Father in the name of our Lord Jesus Christ" (Ephesians 5:20). As I thought on the things I've thanked God for, none can surpass thanking God for God, the Source of my resources: "The Lord is my rock, and my fortress, and my deliverer; my God, my strength, in whom I will trust; my buckler, and the horn of my salvation, and my high tower" (Psalm 18:2).

Being a thankful retired preschool teacher having worked with young children over 27 1/2 years, I've learned it was very important during those early years to introduce preschoolers to their *ABC*'s. To make it easier for the children to recognize the alphabets, one of my methods was to teach the *ABC* song. As the children sang, I pointed out the letters from A to Z. Oh how they would joyfully and enthusiastically sing the song, yet not able to identify the letters! Not knowing the letters didn't deter them from singing; they were just enjoying the learning experience. Little did they know, they were singing about the very foundation of knowing and growing in literature from A to Z. Feeling blessed to have been there for my sister, and having helped mold and taught those little ones, has inspired me to think about the very essence of my gratitude. Reflecting on my life, I realize the source of my gratitude resides in God.

As a child my parents told me who God was, but I didn't know in reality who He really was and would do. Like the children I once taught, I too was enjoying the learning experience, going to Sunday School learning the names and attributes of God; it was fun and exciting! Little did I know, I was reciting and learning about the foundation that would propel me on my Christian journey.

Thanking and praising God through Scripture has kept me grounded in faith. My faith in God, along with the original purpose of this book has motivated me to write. One day while meditating, I thought of Job when he said, "Oh that my words were now written! oh that they were printed in a book! That they were graven with an iron pen and lead in the rock forever!" (Job 19:23-24). I then began to consider my many journals, and jotted pieces of paper. My sister's words hit me like waves beating upon rocks, *"This is the book!"* The words were so clear, I thought she was speaking from the grave (not literally). Now—I know it was God inspiring me to write a book that will inspire (not only sisters), but all people to be grateful to Him for Him. Hopefully, you will journey with me. As a result of our gratitude to God, having *Something to Thank About from A to Z*, I was able to go onward and upwards through Scripture to heights of gratitude I've never known in Him. So will you.

The Good News is

The good news is, since we all know our ABC's, this book will be an easy read. We have 365 days to offer thanksgiving and praises to God for God from A to Z. The Holy Bible says: "But the word is very nigh, unto thee, in thy mouth, and in thy heart, that thou mayest do it" (Deuteronomy 30:14). As you will find the spiritual treasure of knowing God is in His Word. If you dig deep in His Word, you will learn many ways to express gratitude to God for God.

Your gratitude will soar in Christ as you begin to discover who God is, what He has done, is doing, and what He will forever do. Consider the scripture, "Trust in the LORD with all thine heart; and lean not unto thine own understanding" (Proverbs 3:5). Prayerfully and meditatively you will soon realize you can thank God for God, our *Trust*, the *Lord*, our *Leaning Post*, and the *One Who Understands*. Today, I encourage you to ask the Holy Spirit to open your heart to the deeper, yet higher revelations of God found in His Word. God will reveal to you what you have to be thankful for in Him for Him (even on a personal level).

We've all heard people say, "We all have something to pray about." Why not add, "We all have something to thank about?" Have you thanked God for God today? If not, the good news is, it's not too late. Though we are far passed the preschool level of learning, let's start "thanking" on a higher level of knowing. It is far passed time to think thankfully to God for God by using His Word. I assure you, having *Something to Thank About from A to Z*, will open your heart to what you've been longing for in Him. It did for me.

***Special note

At various times throughout this book you will find what I call, *"Plug ins"*. These *"Plug ins"* are my stopping points that express the depth of gratitude we have to God for God. While reading *Something to Thank About from A to Z*, you may have your own thankful *"Plug in"*. It may be found in the A's, B's, C's through the X's, Y's, or Z's. At the end of each chapter opportunity has been provided for you to plug in. Don't hesitate, just decide to stop, pray, meditate, and plug into the Power Source. The Holy Spirit is waiting on you.

"Now therefore, our God, we thank thee, and praise thy glorious name" (1 Chronicles 29:13).

Chapter 1

THANKING and PRAISING GOD for GOD through A, B, C, D, E, F, G

A

ALL IN ALL, *The:* "And when all things shall be subdued unto him, then shall the Son also himself be subject unto him that put all things under him, that God may be all in all."1 Corinthians 15:28

"One God and Father of all, who is above all, and through all, and in you all." Ephesians 4:6

"Where there is neither Greek nor Jew, circumcision nor un-circumcision, Barbarian, Scythian, bond nor free: but Christ is all, and in all." Colossians 3:11

ALL SUFFICIENT: "And God is able to make all grace abound toward you; that ye, always having all sufficiency in all things, may abound to every good work:" 2 Corinthians 9:8

"If I were hungry, I would not tell thee: for the world is mine, and the fullness thereof." Psalm 50:12

ALMIGHTY, *The:* "And when Abraham was ninety years old and nine, the LORD, appeared to Abram, and said unto him, I am the Almighty God; walk before me, and be thou perfect." Genesis 17:1

"The mighty God, even the LORD, hath spoken, and called the earth from the rising of the sun unto the going down thereof." Psalm 50:1

"The LORD on high is mightier than the noise of many waters, yea, than the mighty waves of the sea." Psalm 93:4

The LORD thy God in the midst of thee is mighty; he will save, he will rejoice over thee with joy; he will rest in his love, he will joy over thee with singing." Zephaniah 3:17

Plug in
Why not begin each day thanking God for having all might?
He is the God Almighty; there is no other. We thank Him for being
the absolute authority, invincible, omnipotent, and
supreme God. We praise
Him for being all wise, all good, all powerful, all loving supplying
our every need.

God stands in His omnipotence and sovereignty,
waiting for us to hand
Him our heavy load. As Scripture declares, "For there is nothing
too hard for our Lord."
"Casting all your care on him for he cares for you."
We have the assurance our God is more than able to bear whatever
is too heavy for us.
He is mighty in power and mighty in strength.
He is able to handle everything
that comes our way. We are totally secure in His hand.

God is more than able to carry my load.
God, the Almighty, we say, "thank you."

ALPHA AND OMEGA, *The:* "Saying, I am Alpha and Omega, the first and the last: and, What thou seest, write in a book, and send it unto the seven churches which are in Asia; unto Ephesus, and unto Smyrna, and unto Pergamos, and unto Thyatira, and unto Sardis, and unto Philadelphia, and unto Laodicea." Revelation 1:11

"And he said unto me, It is done. I am Alpha and Omega, the beginning and the end. I will give unto him that is athirst of the fountain of the water of life freely." Revelation 21:6

"I am Alpha and Omega, the beginning and the end, the first and the last." Revelation 22:13

AMEN, *The*: "And unto the angel of the church of the Laodiceans write; These things saith the Amen, the faithful and true witness, the beginning of the creation of God;" Revelation 3:14

Plug in

Lord God, we thank and praise you because you are God,
The Amen.
You stand in agreement with your own self;
Amen.
Your Word is true and faithful;
Amen.
It needs no witness;
Amen.
It can and does stand by its self;
Amen.
It is so, for God said it;
Amen.
Agree to it, for there is none other;
Amen.
There is no doubt about it;
Amen.
He is the faithful and true witness;
Amen.
So be it, for God is;
Amen.

No matter what I say; God has the final say in my life.
God, the Amen, we say, "thank you."

ANCIENT OF DAYS, *The*: "I beheld till the thrones were cast down, and the Ancient of days did sit, whose garment was white as snow, and the hair of his head like the pure wool: his throne was like the fiery flame, and his wheels as burning fire." Daniel 7:9

"I saw in the night visions, and, behold, one like the Son of man came with the clouds of heaven, and came to the Ancient of days, and they brought him near before him. And there was given him dominion and glory, and a kingdom, that all people, nations, and languages, should serve him: his dominion is an everlasting dominion, which shall not pass away, and his kingdom that which shall not be destroyed." Daniel 7:13-14

"I beheld, and the same horn made war with the saints, and prevailed against them; Until the Ancient of days came, and judgment was given to the saints of the most High; and the time came that the saints possessed the kingdom." Daniel 7:21-22

ANSWER IN THE SECRET PLACE OF THUNDER, *The:* "God thundereth marvelously with his voice; great things doeth he, which we cannot comprehend." Job 37:5

"Thou calledst in trouble, and I delivered thee; I answered thee in the secret place of thunder: I proved thee at the waters of Meribah. Selah." Psalm 81:7

"Call unto me, and I will answer thee, and shew thee great and mighty things, which thou knowest not." Jeremiah 33:3

Plug in

Have you ever been in a secret place of thunder?
Perhaps the storm got so intense you dared to tell anyone but God?
After much prayer and praise, to your amazement, God
heard and answered
right out of that secret place of thunder; where the storm was
raging mightily!
While in that secret place of thunder, did you realize
God our Father,
already knew beforehand the storm was coming? Did you consider,
He also knew why the storm was going on, and when it was to end?

I'm reminded of Jacob when he wrestled with the angel
all night long.
He said, "I will not give sleep to mine eyes, or slumber
to mine eyelids until I find a place for the LORD, an habitation
for the mighty God of Jacob." (Psalm 132: 4-5). Jacob refused
to let go until he was blessed. Surely he was in that secret
place of thunder
wrestling with the angel of Lord God Almighty! Like Jacob,
God will answer us and show us great and mighty things
we know not of.

I can never weather the storms by myself; I need God, my
Spiritual Meteorologist.
God, our Answer in the Secret Place of Thunder, we say, "thank you."

AUTHOR, *The:* "For God is not the author of confusion, but of peace, as in all churches of the saints." 1 Corinthians 14:33

"And being made perfect, he became the author *of* eternal salvation unto all them that obey him;" Hebrews 5:9

"Looking unto Jesus the author and finisher of our faith; who for the joy sat before him endured the cross, despising the shame, and is set down at the right hand of the throne of God." Hebrews 12:2

AUTHORITY, *The:* "For he taught them as one having authority, and not as the scribes." Matthew 7:29

"And they were all amazed, insomuch that they questioned among themselves, saying, What thing is this? what new doctrine is this? for with authority commandeth he even the unclean spirits, and they do obey him." Mark 1:27

"Then he called his twelve disciples together, and gave them power and authority over all devils, and to cure diseases." Luke 9:1

AWAKENER, *The:* "The Lord GOD has given me the tongue of the learned, that I should know how to speak a word in season to him that is weary: he wakeneth morning by morning, he wakeneth mine ear to hear as the learned." Isaiah 50:4

"Wherefore he saith, Awake thou sleepest, and arise from the dead, and Christ shall give thee light." Ephesians 5:14

Plug in

Lord, we thank you for waking us this morning, and clothing us in our right mind.
We thank you for giving us the ability to move our limbs as strength increased.
Thank you for waking our ears to hear and eyes to see.
Thank you for maintaining the constant beat of our hearts, and the flow of our breaths.

We realize you are the reason we woke up this morning.
You are the reason we opened our eyes.
You are the reason our hearts kept beatings, and
You are the reason we're still alive.

Thank you for waking us to see another beautiful God designed day.
Thank you for assigning something for us to do, learn, share, help, touch, give, and love. Thank you for giving us opportunities
to tell others about Jesus, the truth, the life, and the way.

Everyday my God wakes me, both physically and spiritually.
God, our Awakener, we say, "thank you."

AVENGER, *The:* "To me belongeth vengeance, and recompence; their foot shall slide in due time: for the day of their calamity is at hand, and the things that shall come upon them make haste." Deuteronomy 32:35

"The LORD judge between me and thee, and the LORD avenge me of thee: but mine hand shall not be upon thee." I Samuel 24:12

"It is God that avengeth me, and subdueth the people under me." Psalm 18:47

"O LORD God, to whom vengeance belongeth; O God, to whom vengeance belongeth, shew thyself." Psalm 94:1

"Dearly beloved, avenge not yourselves, but rather give place unto wrath: for it is written, Vengeance is mine; I will repay, said the Lord." Romans 12:19

Plug in

This seem to be a most difficult thing to do at times, giving place to wrath.
We often find ourselves instead, reacting to the wrath.
How does one give place to wrath? Personally, I can't answer that question for you.
But I can say what the Bible says, "...let every man be swift to hear, slow to speak,
slow to wrath: for the wrath of man worketh not the righteousness of God."

Wrath shouldn't become a reaction for us. Instead let's give glory to God
by giving time in prayer, meditation, confession, and thankfulness.
Remember God doesn't forget when we refuse to retaliate.
Father God, we thank and give you praise because vengeance belongs to you.
You will repay.

Since vengeance belongs to God, I have no need to retaliate.
God, our Avenger, we say, "thank you."

B

BEAUTIFIER, *The*: "Honor and majesty are before him: strength and beauty are in his sanctuary." Psalm 96:6

"O worship the LORD in the beauty of holiness. Fear before him, all the earth." Psalm 96:9

"For the LORD taketh pleasure in his people; He will beautify the meek with salvation." Psalm 149:4

"He hath made every thing beautiful in his time: also he hath set the world in their heart, so that no man can find out the work that God maketh from the beginning to the end." Ecclesiastes 3:11

BLESSER, *The:* "The LORD bless thee, and keep thee: The LORD make his face shine upon thee, and be gracious unto thee: The LORD lift up his countenance upon thee, and give thee peace. And they shall put my name upon the children of Israel; and I will bless them." Numbers 6:24-27

"Behold, I have received commandment to bless: and he hath blessed; and I cannot reverse it." Numbers 23:20

"For thou, LORD, wilt bless the righteous; with favour wilt thou compass him as with a shield." Psalm 5:12

"Then shall the earth yield her increase; and God, even our own God, shall bless us. God shall bless us; and all the ends of the earth shall fear him." Psalms 67:6-7

"Blessed be the God and Father of our Lord Jesus Christ, who has blessed us with all spiritual blessings in heavenly places in Christ:" Ephesians 1:3

BOUNDARY SETTER, *The:* "And Moses said unto the LORD, The people cannot come up to mount Sinai: for thou chargedst us, saying, Set bounds about the mount, and sanctify it." Exodus 19: 23

"When he gave to the sea his decree, that the waters should not pass his commandment: When he appointed the foundations of the earth:" Proverbs 8:28

"Fear ye not me? said the LORD: will ye not tremble at my presence, which have placed the sand for the bound of the sea by a perpetual decree, that it cannot pass it: and though the waves thereof toss themselves, yet can they not prevail; though they roar, yet can they not pass over it?" Jeremiah 5:22

Plug in

Father, we thank you for setting boundaries for us.
We are grateful you're not setting these boundaries for him, but to help us
stay within a place of safety.
We realize you have a stopping point that we cannot cross.
We can only go so far; in our own self
we are restricted. Just like the waves of the sea,
we thank you for keeping us within bounds.
Though at times we may roar,
please help us to stay within the perimeter set for us.
Every time we attempt to go out of your boundaries,
we fall on our faces.
Sometimes we bump our head and scrape our knees.
At other times we break our hearts in pieces.
Lord, help us to stop when we see clearly your stop sign.
You are the One in control.

**It didn't matter how I felt, or how I wanted to continue on;
when God brought me to His stop sign, I had to stop.**
God, our Boundary Setter, we say, "thank you."

BREAD OF HEAVEN, *The*: "The people asked, and he brought quails, and satisfied them with the bread of heaven." Psalm 105:40

"Then Jesus said unto them, Verily, verily, I say unto you, Moses gave you not that bread from heaven; but my Father giveth you the true bread from heaven. For the bread of God is he which cometh down from heaven, and giveth life unto the world." John 6:32-33

"And Jesus said unto them, I am the bread of Life; he that cometh to me shall never hunger; and he that believeth on me shall never thirst." John 6:35

"I am that bread of life." John 6:48

"I am the living bread which came down from heaven: if any man eat of this bread, he shall live for ever: and the bread that I will give is my flesh, which I will give for the life of the world." John 6:51

BRIGHT AND MORNING STAR, *The*: "At the brightness that was before him his thick clouds passed, hail stones and coals of fire." Psalm 18:12

"Who being the brightness of his glory, and the express image of his person, and upholding all things by the word of his power, when he had by himself purged our sins, sat down on the right hand of the Majesty on high;" Hebrews 1:3

"I Jesus have sent mine angel to testify unto you these things in the churches. I am the root and the offspring of David, and the bright and morning star." Revelation 22:16

Plug in

As many have said, there is a brighter day ahead.
When we all get to heaven what a day of rejoicing that will be!
But thanks be to God through Jesus, we can rejoice right now.
For to be in the very presence of the brightness of His glory
fill our hearts with joy and gladness.
We are thankful we don't have to reside in darkness any longer;
the Light has come!
With Him there is no night or day. They both are alike to Him.
Christ in us is the brightness of His glory, and the express
image of His person.
He holds everything by the word of His power,
and is now sitting down on the right hand of the Majesty on high,
and still shining.

No matter how dark it seemed to be,
every morning God's bright light kept shining through.
God, our Bright and Morning Star, we say, "thank you."

BUILDER, *The:* "O LORD our God, all this store that we have prepared to build thee an house for thine holy name cometh of thine hand, and is all thine own." 1 Chronicles 29:16

"EXCEPT the LORD build the house, they labour in vain that build it: except the LORD keep the city, the watchman waketh but in vain." Psalm 127:1

"In whom all the building fitly framed together growth unto an holy temple in the Lord: In whom ye also are builded together for an habitation of God through the Spirit." Ephesians 2:21-22

"For every house is builded by some man; but he that built all things is God." Hebrews 3:4

"For he looked for a city which hath foundation, whose builder and maker is God." Hebrews 11:10

Plug in

Dear Lord, we thank you our Builder.
Thank you for building our physical and spiritual house.
Thank you for knowing what lumber, nails, plaster,
and screws to use.
Build us, O Lord, that our lumber may be a wall against the storm;
our planks may be strong, and
our nails may be those that are fastened to your cross.
Build us that our screws may be tightened to secure what we
have in you, and
our plaster may be applied smooth to cover the rough
edges of our frame.
Though storm rises and wind blows,
we are assured that everyone knows
the house built on the rock of Christ will stand.

God kept my house standing and my home together.
God, our Builder, we say, "thank you."

C

CALLER, *Our:* "And we know that all things work together for good to them that love God, to them who are the called according to his purpose." Romans 8:28

"(For the children being not yet born, neither having done any good or evil, that the purpose of God according to election might stand, not of works, but of him that callest;)" Romans 9:11

"Even us, whom he hath called, and not of the Jews only, but also of the Gentiles?" Romans 9:24

"For, brethren, ye have been called unto liberty; only use not liberty for an occasion to the flesh, but by love serve one another." Galatians 5:13

"Who hath saved us, and called us with an holy calling, not according to our works, but according to his own purpose and grace, which was given us in Christ Jesus before the world began," 2 Timothy 1:9

CHAIN RELEASER, *Our:* "God setteth the solitary in families: he bringeth out those which are bound with chains: but the rebellious dwell in a dry land." Psalm 68:6

"He brought them out of darkness and the shadow of death, and brake their bands in sunder." Psalm 107:14

"O LORD, truly I am thy servant; I am thy servant, and the son of thine handmaid: thou hast loosed my bonds." Psalm 116:16

"The Spirit of the Lord GOD is upon me; because the LORD hath anointed me to preach good tidings unto the meek; he hath sent me to bind up the brokenhearted, to proclaim liberty to the captives, and the opening of the prison to them that are bound;" Isaiah 61:1

Plug in

It was God who brought
the Israelites out of darkness and the shadow of death.
He broke their chains in pieces. God is still that God.
He has not changed. He's still breaking chains in Jesus' name.
God breaks not only physical chains, but the spiritual chains
that hold us down:
The chains of envy, jealousy, bitterness, and strife,
which should never be part of the Christian life.

Thank you Lord, for releasing us from that which binds,
immobilizes, shackles, and holds us separated from you.
Lord, break that chain;
break that chain that we may see.
Please dear Lord, break that chain in me.

The chain that had me down, God broke it.
God, our Chain Releaser, we say, "thank you."

CHANGER, *Our*: "Behold, I shew you a mystery; We shall not all sleep, but we shall all be changed, In a moment, in the twinkling of an eye, at the last trump: for the trumpet shall sound, and the dead shall be raised incorruptible, and we shall be changed." 1 Corinthians 15:51-52

"For our conversation is in heaven; from whence also we look for the Saviour, the Lord Jesus Christ: Who shall change our vile body, that it may be fashioned like unto his glorious body, according to the working whereby he is able even to subdue all things unto himself." Philippians 3:20-21

CHASTISER, *Our:* "Behold, happy is the man whom God correcteth: therefore despise not thou the chastening of the Almighty:" Job 5:17

"He that chastiseth the heathen, shall not he correct? he that teacheth man knowledge, shall not he know? Psalm 94:10

"The LORD hath chastened me sore: but he hath not given me over unto death." Psalm 118:18

"My son, despise not the chastening of the LORD: neither be weary of his correction: For whom the LORD loveth he correcteth; even as a father the son in whom he delighteth." Proverbs 3:11-12

"For whom the Lord loveth he chasteneth, and scourgeth every son whom he receiveth." Hebrews 12:6

"Furthermore we have had fathers of our flesh which corrected us, and we gave them reverence: shall we not much rather be in subjection unto the Father of spirits, and live?" Hebrew 12:9

Plug in

Father, we thank and praise you for being our Chastiser.
Lord, help us to realize it's high time we stop trying to chastise
our sisters and brothers for the so-called wrong
we think they are doing. Help us to stop trying to make people
the way we want them to be. Help us to leave that to you.
Thank you for showing us that only you can
fix the so-called unfixable, shape the so-called un-shapeable;
move the so-called un-moveable, and save the so-called un-savable.
Please help us to appreciate and rest in your way of discipline.

Though it may hurt my ego, I'm glad God corrects me;
He knows when, where, and how; He makes no mistakes.
God, our Chastiser, we say, "thank you."

COMFORTER, *Our:* "I, even I, am he that comforteth you: who art thou, that thou shouldest be afraid of a man that shall die, and of the son of man which shall be made as grass;" Isaiah 51:12

"I will not leave you comfortless: I will come to you." John 14:18

"Blessed be God, even the Father of our Lord Jesus Christ, the Father of mercies, and the God of all comfort;" 2 Corinthians 1:3

"If there be therefore any consolation in Christ, if any comfort of love, if any fellowship of the Spirit, if any bowels and mercies, Fulfil ye my joy, that ye be likeminded having the same love, being of one accord, of one mind." Philippians 2:1-2

"Now our Lord Jesus Christ himself, and God, even our Father, which hath loved us, and hath given us everlasting consolation and good hope through grace, Comfort your hearts, and stablish you in every good word and work." 2 Thessalonians 2:16-17

Plug in

Father God, we thank and praise you for comforting us.
Help us to follow Christ's example and comfort someone else.
We are aware there are so many sad, lonely, and hurting people
who could benefit from a word of comfort. You have shown
that a smile, hug, word, or deed can reach deep into a lonely heart.
We thank you for giving us a smile to brighten someone's day;
sharing a hug to feel your embrace;
and providing a word or gift to help in time of need.
Lord, we thank you for your loving care,
and the opportunity to share in this consolation.
Help us to comfort someone today.

When I comfort someone else, I too am comforted.
God, our Comforter, we say, "thank you."

COMMANDER, *Our:* "And Moses and Aaron did so, as the LORD commanded; and he lifted up the rod, and smote the waters that were in the river, in the sight of Pharaoh, and in the sight of his servants; and all the waters that were in the river were turned to blood." Exodus 7:20

"Have not I commanded thee? Be strong and of a good courage; be not afraid, neither be thou dismayed: for the LORD thy God is with thee whithersoever thou goest." Joshua 1:9

"Let all the earth fear the LORD: let all the inhabitants of the world stand in awe of him. For he spake, and it was done: he commanded, and it stood fast." Psalm 33:8-9

"Let them praise the name of the LORD: for he commanded, and they were created." Psalm 148:5

"Blessed are they that do his commandments, that they may have right to the tree of life, and may enter in through the gates into the city." Revelation 22:14

COMPASSIONATE: "But he, being full of compassion, forgave their iniquity, and destroyed them not: yea, many a time turned he his anger away, and did not stir up all his wrath." Psalm 78:38

"But thou, O Lord, art a God full of compassion, and gracious, long-suffering, and plenteous in mercy and truth." Psalm 86:15

"And Jesus went forth, and saw a great multitude, and was moved with compassion toward them, and he healed their sick." Matthew 14:14

"And Jesus, moved with compassion, put forth his hand, and touched him, and said unto him, I will; be thou clean." Mark 1:41

CONSUMING FIRE, *A:* "For the LORD thy God is a consuming fire, even a jealous God." Deuteronomy 4:24

"Then the fire of the LORD fell, and consumed the burnt sacrifice, and the wood, and the stones, and the dust, and licked up the water that was in the trench. And when all the people saw it, they fell on their faces: and they said, The LORD, he is the God; the LORD, he is the God." 1 Kings 18:38-39

"Then I said, I will not make mention of him, nor speak any more in his name. But his word was in mine heart as a burning fire shut up in my bones, and I was weary with forbearing, and I could not stay." Jeremiah 20: 9

"Is not my word like as a fire? Saith the LORD; and like a hammer that breaketh the rock in pieces?" Jeremiah 23:29

"For our God is a consuming fire." Hebrews 12:29

CONQUERER, *The:* "And he said, Hearken ye, all Judah, and ye inhabitants of Jerusalem, and thou king Jehoshaphat, Thus saith the LORD unto you, Be not afraid nor dismayed by reason of this great multitude; for the battle is not yours, but God's." 2 Chronicles 20:15

"Nay, in all these things we are more than conquerors through him that loved us." Romans 8:37

"Finally, my brethren, be strong in the Lord, and in the power of his might." Ephesians 6:10

COVERER, *Our:* "Blessed is he whose transgression is forgiven, whose sin is covered." Psalm 32:1

"He shall cover thee with his feathers, and under his wings shalt thou trust: his truth shall be thy shield and buckler." Psalm 91:4

"O God the Lord, the strength of my salvation, thou hast covered my head in the day of battle." Psalm 140:7

"Who covereth the heaven with clouds, who prepareth rain for the earth, who maketh grass to grow upon the mountains. "Psalm 147:8

"Saying, Blessed are they whose iniquities are forgiven, and whose sins are covered." Romans 4:7

Plug in

Aren't we thankful to know God has us covered?
Not with sheets on our beds,
Or with hats on our heads;
But by His blood which He shed.
He has us covered with His unique and wonderful covering;
He covers us gently with His feathers.
He has safely tucked us away
Under His wings until our dying day.
The Lord has covered us from our head to our feet,
In Him to be totally complete.
He has covered our sins by way of His cross,
That none who accepts Him would ever be lost.

God keeps me covered in every way, all the way.
God our Coverer, we say, "thank you".

CREATOR, *The:* "In the beginning God created the heaven and the earth." Genesis 1:1

"So God created man in his own image, in the image of God created he him; male and female created he them." Genesis 1:27

"For, behold, I create new heavens and a new earth: and the former shall not be remembered, nor come into mind." Isaiah 65:17

"Thou, even thou, art LORD alone; thou hast made heaven, the heaven of heavens, with all their host, the earth, and all things that are therein, the seas, and all that is therein, and thou preservest them all; and the host of heaven worshippeth thee." Nehemiah 9:6

"For by him were all things created, that are in heaven, and that are in earth, visible and invisible, whether they be thrones, or dominions, or principalities, or powers: all things were created by him, and for him:" Colossians 1:16

D

DEFENCE, *Our*: "My defence is of God, which saveth the upright in heart." Psalm 7:10

"Bow down thine ear to me; deliver me speedily: be thou my strong rock, for an house of defence to save me." Psalm 31:2

"He only is my rock and my salvation; he is my defence; I shall not be greatly moved." Psalm 62:2

"For the LORD is our defence; and the Holy One of Israel is our king." Psalm 89:18

DELIVERER, *Our:* "All my bones shall say, LORD, who is like unto thee, which deliverest the poor from him that is too strong for him, yea, the poor and the needy from him that spoileth him?" Psalm 35:10

"And call upon me in the day of trouble: I will deliver thee, and thou shalt glorify me." Psalm 50:15

"For thou hast delivered my soul from death, mine eyes from tears, and my feet from falling." Psalm 116:8

"Be not afraid of their faces, for I am with thee to deliver thee, saith the LORD." Jeremiah 1:8

"Who hath delivered us from the power of darkness, and hath translated us into the kingdom of his dear Son:" Colossians 1:13

Plug in

Father God, we thank you for your delivering power.
Thank you for recuing us from the one that was too strong for us.
Thank you for securing our life, wiping our tears away,
and helping us to remain standing.
Oh Lord, we know if you hadn't been on our side,
we would have been swallowed up quick.
Thank you for delivering us from death,
our eyes for tears, and our feet from falling;
and thank you for delivering us
from the power of darkness
to live eternally in your kingdom.

God has delivered me from hell.
God, our Deliverer, we say, "thank you."

DIRECTOR, *Our:* "Order my steps in your word: and let not any iniquity have dominion over me." Psalm 119:133

"In all thy ways acknowledge him; and he shall direct thy paths." Proverbs 3:6

"For the LORD shall be thy confidence, and shall keep thy foot from being taken." Proverbs 3:26

"A man's heart deviseth his way: but the LORD directeth his steps." Proverbs 16: 9.

"And the Lord direct your hearts unto the love of God, and into the patient waiting for Christ." 2 Thessalonians 3:5

Plug in

*Lord, thank you for being our Director. Please help us to wait
on your direction no matter how long it takes.
This can seem hard at times, but I dare us to wait.
Why not ask God to direct our waiting?
He knows the way of waiting in Him.
Thank Him for knowing what steps to take.
Surely He knows the first, the next, and the last.
Just acknowledge Him and follow His lead;
He knows the path we need.*

*If you're planning on going somewhere today;
don't get in a hurry, just wait.
Ask God to direct your steps according to His will.
Lord, we ask you to direct our steps,
our path, and our hearts into your love.
We ask you to direct us into the patience of waiting for Christ.*

God directing my steps, keeps me from tripping.
God, our Director, we say, "thank you."

DOER, *Our:* "This is the LORD's doing, it is marvellous in our eyes." Psalm 118:23

"Now unto him that is able to do exceeding abundantly above all that we ask or think, according to the power that worketh in us, Unto him be glory in the church by Christ Jesus throughout all ages, world without end." Amen." Ephesians 3:20-21

"I am the vine, ye are the branches: He that abideth in me, and I in him, the same bringeth forth much fruit: for without me ye can do nothing." John 15:5

"Faithful is he that calleth you, who also will do it." 1 Thessalonians 5:24

DRAWER OF MEN, *The*: "He sent from above, he took me, he drew me out of many waters." Psalm 18:16

"No man can come to me, except the Father which hath sent me draw him: and I will raise him up at the last day." John 6:44

"And I, if I be lifted up from the earth, will draw all men unto me." John 12:32

Plug in

Father, we're grateful your Word says,
if you be lifted up from the earth,
you'll draw all men unto yourself.
We thank and praise you for drawing us to you.
We thank you for sending, taking,
and drawing us out of many waters.
You saw we were drowning in sin,
and didn't know how to swim to safety.
We didn't even know how to take hold of your hand.
Thank you for taking us from the dangerous waters of
depression, desperation, and despair;
hardness, helplessness, and hopelessness;
high-mindedness and hatred.
Thank you for being right there, our rescuer, our lifeline.
Oh, how many waters have you drawn us out from!
We can never name them all, but we can rejoice and say,
"Thank you Lord for grabbing on to me."

God has been my lifeline all along.
God, the Drawer of All Men, we say, "thank you.".

DWELLING PLACE, *Our:* "LORD, thou hast been our dwelling place in all generations." Psalm 90:1

"He that dwelleth in the secret place of the most High shall abide under the shadow of the Almighty." Psalms 91:1

"Because thou hast made the LORD, which is my refuge, even the most High, thy habitation; There shall no evil befall thee, neither shall any plague come nigh thy dwelling." Psalm 91:9-10

"And we have known and believed the love that God hath to us. God is love; and he that dwelleth in love dwelleth in God, and God in him." 1 John 4:16

Plug in

Lord, thank you for being our dwelling place.
Thank you for providing a place we can call home;
A place to lay our head to abide in you alone.
Never to be separate; always together;
You are our dwelling place in any kind of weather.
To dwell with you from all hurt and harm,
There can never be need for alarm.
We are thankful to be safe in your loving arm.

When it felt like the wind was about to blow the roof off,
God kept me secure under His arm.
God, our Dwelling Place, we say, "thank you."

E

ENEMY SLAYER, *The*: "But if thou shalt indeed obey his voice, and do all that I speak; then I will be an enemy unto thine enemies, and an adversary unto thine adversaries." Exodus 23:22

"The LORD shall cause thine enemies that rise up against thee to be smitten before thy face: they shall come out against thee one way, and flee before thee seven ways." Deuteronomy 28:7

"O thou enemy, destructions are come to a perpetual end: and thou hast destroyed cities; their memorial is perished with them." Psalm 9:6

"Through God we shall do valiantly: for he it is that shall tread down our enemies." Psalm 60:12

"And that he might reconcile both unto God in one body by the cross having slain the enmity thereby." Ephesians 2:16

Plug in

Do we know who the enemy is; who he really is?
It's not our mother or our father, nor husband or wife.
It's not our brother or sister, nor friend or associate.
It's not even our boss or coworker. Then who is this enemy?
The enemy is Satan. Sometimes he's hard to recognize
because he works from the inside to wreak havoc without.
But thanks be to God we have an Enemy Slayer, who has slain
the enemy on the cross by the precious blood of Jesus!
The enemy is defeated, and we must believe it!

**The enemy can't knock me out anymore;
God has won all the rounds.**
God, our Enemy Slayer, we say, "thank you."

ESCAPE MAKER, *Our*: "Our soul is escaped as a bird out of the snare of the fowlers: the snare is broken, and we are escaped." Psalm 124:7

"Therefore they sought again to take him: but he escaped out of their hand," John 10:39

"There hath no temptation taken you but such as common to man: but God is faithful, who will not suffer you to be tempted above that ye are able; but will with the temptation also make a way to escape, that ye may be able to bare it." I Corinthians 10:13

Plug in

Have you ever found yourself in the grips or
clutches of Satan?
Literally, was he squeezing you so tight you felt as if you were
going to explode?
All you wanted was a way out; to get away;
a second chance.
You looked around and up and down
for a way to escape; there seemed to be none.
But thanks be to God for God;
He provides a way of escape for His children.

I'm reminded how God provided a way of escape for David out
of the hand of King Saul. It was God protecting David by having
Michal (David's wife, Saul's daughter) to let David down through
a window, escaping the hand of Saul (1 Samuel 19:12). It was
God who made a way of escape for Saul of Tarsus, by leading His
disciples to let him down by the wall in a basket, escaping the Jews
at Damascus (2 Corinthians 11:33). What a mighty God we serve!
In God's own amazing and unique way there it was—a way out of
the trap of Satan!
We too can give praises to God for providing His own way
of escape for us.
Let's thank God for His unique, "Escape Hatch."

I am no longer trapped behind Satan's bars;
God has provided my way of escape.
God, our Escape Maker, we say, "thank you."

ESTABLISHER, *Our*: "Oh let the wickedness of the wicked come to an end; but establish the just: for the righteous God trieth the hearts and reins." Psalm 7:9

"He brought me up also out of an horrible pit, out of the miry clay, and set my feet upon a rock, and established my goings." Psalm 40:2

"And let the beauty of the LORD our God be upon us: and establish thou the work of our hands upon us; yea, the work of our hands establish thou it." Psalm 90:17

"Now he which stablisheth us with you in Christ, and hath anointed us, is God;" 2 Corinthians 1:21

"To the end he may stablish your hearts unblameable in holiness before God, even our Father, at the coming of our Lord Jesus Christ with all his saints." 1 Thessalonians 3:13

ETERNAL: "The LORD shall reign for ever and ever." Exodus 15:18

"For thus saith the high and lofty One that inhabitedth eternity, whose name is Holy; I dwell in the high and lofty place, with him also that is of a contrite and humble spirit, to revive the spirit of the humble, and to revive the heart of the contrite ones." Isaiah 57:15

"But the God of all grace, who has called us into his eternal glory by Christ Jesus, after that ye have suffered a while, make you perfect, stablish, strengthen, settle you." 1 Peter 5:10

"And this is the record, that God hath given to us eternal life, and this life is in his Son." 1 John 5:11

EVERLASTING GOD, *The:* "And Abraham planted a grove in Beersheba, and called there on the name of the LORD, the everlasting God." Genesis 21:33

"Blessed be the LORD God of Israel from everlasting, and to everlasting. Amen, and Amen." Psalm 41:13

"Before the mountains were brought forth, or ever thou hadst formed the earth and the world, even from everlasting to everlasting, thou art God." Psalms 90:2

"Thy throne is established of old: thou art from everlasting." Psalm 93:2

EXALTED, *The:* "Thine, O LORD, is the greatness, and the power, and the glory, and the victory, and the majesty: for all that is in the heaven and in the earth is thine; thine is the kingdom, O LORD, and thou art exalted as head above all." 1 Chronicles 29: 11

"O magnify the LORD with me, and let us exalt his name together." Psalm 34:3

"Let all those that seek thee rejoice and be glad in thee: let such as love thy salvation say continually, The LORD be magnified." Psalm 40:16

"Be thou exalted, O God, above the heavens: and thy glory above all the earth;" Psalm 108:5

EXCELLENT: "O LORD, our Lord, how excellent is thy name in all the earth! who hast set thy glory above the heavens." Psalm 8:1

"Thou art more glorious and excellent than the mountains of prey." Psalm 76:4

"Let them praise the name of the LORD: for his name alone is excellent; his glory is above the earth and heaven." Psalm 148:13

"Praise him for his mighty acts: praise him according to his excellent greatness." Psalm 150:2

"Have not I written unto you excellent things in counsels and knowledge," Proverbs 22:20

"But we have this treasure in earthen vessels, that the excellency of the power may be of God, and not of us." 2 Corinthians 4:7

Plug in

*O Lord, our Lord, we thank and give you praise for
you are Excellent!
Lord, how can we understand the depth and height, length and width, of
your majesty in all your excellency!
O Lord, we humbly bow to you.
Your wisdom surpasses all.
Your glory exalts itself with the very essence of
your creation. In your excellency,
O Lord, your Majesty, we glorify thee.*

**Through the excellence of His power,
I am raised to praise His name.**
God, whose name alone is Excellent, we say, "thank you."

EYE OPENER, *Our:* "And Elisha prayed, and said, LORD, I pray thee, open his eyes, that he may see. And the LORD opened the eyes of the young man; and he saw: and, behold, the mountain was full of horses and chariots of fire round about Elisha." 2 Kings 6:17

"The LORD openeth the eyes of the blind: The LORD raiseth them that are bowed down: The LORD loveth the righteous:" Psalm 146:8

"And Jesus said unto him, Receive thy sight: thy faith hath saved thee." Luke 18:42

"Therefore said they unto him, How were thine eyes opened? He answered and said, A man that is called Jesus made clay, and anointed mine eyes, and said unto me, Go to the pool of Siloam, and wash: and I went and washed, and I received sight." John 9:10-11

F

FAITHFUL: "Know therefore that the LORD thy God, he is God, the faithful God, which keepeth covenant and mercy with them that love him and keep his commandments to a thousand generations;" Deuteronomy 7:9

"It is of the LORD's mercies that we are not consumed, because his compassions fail not. They are new every morning: Great is thy faithfulness." Lamentations 3:23-24

"God is faithful, by whom ye were called unto the fellowship of his Son Jesus Christ our Lord." 1 Corinthians 1:9

"In whom we have boldness and access with confidence by the faith of him." Ephesians 3:12

"Let us hold fast the profession of our faith without wavering; (for he is faithful that promised;)" Hebrews 10:23

Plug in

Father, we thank you because you are Faithful.
Every day we see evidence of your faithfulness.
Your whole creation speaks. The moon and the stars shine every night.
Your sun rises every day. Your wind blows and your grass grows.
Every step we take is in response to your faithfulness.
Every merciful and compassionate act granted
is the result of your faithfulness;
they are new every morning.

God's faithfulness never goes flat;
it continually brings me through every day.
God, the Faithful, we say, "thank you."

FATHER, *Our:* "A father of the fatherless, and a judge of the widows, is God in his holy habitation." Psalm 68:5

"But now, O LORD, thou art our Father; we are the clay, and thou our potter; and we all are the work of thy hand." Isaiah 64:8

"After this manner therefore pray ye: Our Father which art in heaven. Hallowed be thy name." Matthew 6:9

"Every good gift and every perfect gift is from above, and cometh down from the Father of lights, with whom is no variableness, neither shadow of turning." James 1:17

FAULTLESS: "Then said Pilate to the chief priests and to the people, I find no fault in this man." Luke 23:4

"When the chief priests therefore and officers saw him, they cried out, saying, Crucify him, crucify him. Pilate saith unto them, Take ye him, and crucify him: for I find no fault in him." John 19:6

"How much more shall the blood of Christ, who through the eternal Spirit offered himself without spot to God, purge your conscience from dead works to serve the living God?" Hebrews 9:14

"Now unto him that is able to keep you from falling, and to present you faultless before the presence of his glory with exceeding joy, To the only wise God our Saviour, be glory and majesty, dominion and power, both now and ever. Amen." Jude 1:24-25

Plug in

Father, we thank and praise you the Faultless God.
We thank you for taking on sin for us
in the person of our Lord and Savior Jesus Christ,
yet without fault.
It is written in your Word you didn't do anything wrong.
You took our wrongness and put it on you,
yet without fault.
When yelled at and ridiculed, you didn't argue back.
Though carried from judgment hall to judgment hall,
you chose not to say a mumbling word.
yet without fault.
You were lied on and spat on;
A crown of thorns placed around your head,
You were whipped all night long;
still no fault found.
Pieced in your side and nailed to the cross,
Crucified for me and you;
still no fault found.
Now, all thanks to you for keeping us from falling,
that one day before your glory and abundant joy,
you will present us with
no fault found.

When I confess my sins, God wipes my slate clean every time.
God, the Faultless God, we say, "thank you."

FEEDER, *The:* "Which executeth judgment for the oppressed: which giveth food to the hungry. The LORD looseth the prisoners:" Psalm 146:7

"He giveth to the beast his food, and to the young ravens which cry." Psalm 147:9

"Remove far from me vanity and lies: give me neither poverty nor riches; feed me with food convenient for me:" Proverbs 30:8

"He that hath an ear, let him hear what the Spirit saith unto the churches; To him that overcometh will I give to eat of the hidden manna, and will give him a white stone, and in the stone a new name written, which no man knoweth saving he that receiveth it." Revelation 2:17

FIGHTER, *Our:* "The LORD shall fight for you, and ye shall hold your peace." Exodus 14:14

"And took off their chariot wheels, that they drave them heavily: so that the Egyptians said, Let us flee from the face of Israel; for the LORD fighteth for them against the Egyptians." Exodus 14:25

"The LORD your God which goeth before you, he shall fight for you, according to all that he had did for you in Egypt before your eyes;" Deuteronomy 1:30

"In what place therefore ye hear the sound of the trumpet resort ye thither unto us: our God shall fight for us: So we laboured in the work: and half of them held the spears from the rising of the morning till the stars appeared." Nehemiah 4:20-21

"Then he answered and spake unto me, saying, This is the word of the LORD unto Zerubbabel, saying, Not by might, nor by power, but by my spirit, saith the LORD of hosts." Zechariah 4:6

Plug in

Have you ever seen sheep fighting in their own strength?
We are God's sheep and we have no strength for battling.
God desires us only to fight the good fight of faith.
Sometime we must get up, get dressed, and go to the battle field;
God is on the battle field with us.
If there's to be any fighting, God is well equipped
to get the job done
according to His perfect will and skill.
Just as the Lord said to Zerubbabel,
"Not by might, nor by power, but by my spirit,
saith the LORD of hosts."

Although God is our Fighter, He still expects
every soldier of His to be armed
and ready for battle. He said for us to "put on the whole armour of
God, that ye may be able to stand against the wiles of the devil."
It has been proven through Scripture, time after time,
only God can put the enemy to flight. Our fight is our faith. Please
note, God did not call us to fight the enemy. We must submit to God,
resist the devil, and he will flee from us.

When I humble myself and resists the devil,
it is God that makes him run.
God, our Fighter, we say, "thank you."

FIRST AND THE LAST, *The*: "Who hath wrought and done it, calling the generations from the beginning? I the LORD, the first, and with the last: I am he." Isaiah 41:4

"Thus saith the LORD the King of Israel, and his redeemer the LORD of hosts; I am the first, and I am the last, and beside me there is no God." Isaiah 44:6

"And when I saw him, I fell at his feet as dead. And he laid his right hand upon me, saying unto me, Fear not; I am the first and the last:" Revelation 1:17

FORGIVER OF SINS, *The:* "I acknowledged my sin unto thee, and mine iniquity have I not hid. I said, I will confess my transgressions unto the LORD; and thou forgavest the iniquity of my sin. Selah." Psalm 32:5

"For thou, Lord, art good, and ready to forgive; and plenteous in mercy unto all them that call upon thee." Psalm 86:5

"And forgive our debts, as we forgive our debtors." Matthew 6:12

"And when he saw their faith, he said unto him, "Man, thy sins are forgiven thee." Luke 5:20

"If we confess our sins, he is faithful and just to forgive us our sins, and to cleanse us from all unrighteousness." 1 John 1:9

Plug in

Forgive, forgive, forgive,
That's the way to live.
If you will—to forgive,
God will—help you.

Lord, we are grateful you are the forgiver of our sins
through the precious blood of Jesus.
We acknowledge and confess our sins to you.
Thank you for being faithful and just to forgive us.
Thank you for making it possible for us to forgive others.

Hanging on to un-forgiveness is not an option for me;
I must forgive.
God, our Forgiver, we say, "thank you."

FREER, *Our:* "The Spirit of the Lord is upon me, because he hath anointed me to preach the gospel to the poor; he hath sent me to heal the broken hearted, to preach deliverance to the captives, and recovering of sight to the blind, to set at liberty them that are bruised. To preach the acceptable year of the Lord." Luke 4:18-19

"And ye shall know the truth, and the truth shall make you free." John 8:32

"If the Son therefore shall make you free, ye shall be free indeed." John 8:36

"For the law of the Spirit of life in Christ Jesus hath made me free from the law of sin and death." Romans 8:2

"As free, and not using your liberty for a cloak of maliciousness, but as the servants of God." 1 Peter 2:16

G

GIVER, *Our*: "What shall I render unto the LORD for all his benefits toward me? Psalm 116:12

"For God so loved the world, that he gave his only begotton Son, that whosoever believeth in him should not perish, but have everlasting life." John 3:16

"And God, which knoweth the hearts bare them witness, giving them the Holy Ghost, even as he did unto us;" Acts 15:8

"For I would that all men were even as I myself. But every man hath his proper gift of God, one after this manner, and another after that." 1 Corinthians 7:7

"Thanks be unto God for his unspeakable gift." 2 Corinthians 9:15

"If any of you lack wisdom, let him ask of God, that givest to all men liberally, and upbraidest not; and it shall be given him." James 1:5

"But he giveth more grace. Wherefore he saith, God resisteth the proud, but giveth grace unto the humble." James 4: 6

Plug in

Father God, we thank you our Giver.
You loved us so much that you gave all you had.
You gave your only begotten Son that no matter who we are,
if we believe in you, we will live eternally in your kingdom.
We are grateful you made it possible
that we might have a right to this tree of life.

Thank you for giving us your Holy Spirit,
that bears witness with our spirit of this great gift of grace.
Thank you for giving us spiritual gifts,
and the wisdom to use them for your glory and praise.
Lord, help us to embrace what you so freely gave.

I didn't earn, make, or create anything; all I have God gave.
God, our Giver, we say, "thank you."

GLORIFIED, GLORIFIER, GLORIOUS, *The:* "Not unto us, O LORD, not unto us, but unto thy name give glory, for thy mercy, and for thy truth's sake." Psalm 115:1

"Let your light so shine before men, that they may see your good works, and glorify your Father which is in heaven." Matthew 5:16:

"And lead us not into temptation, but deliver us from evil: For thine is the kingdom, and the power, and the glory, for ever, Amen." Matthew 6:13

"These words spake Jesus, and lifted up his eyes to heaven, and said, Father, the hour is come; glorify thy Son, that thy Son also may glorify thee:" John 17:1

"I have glorified thee on the earth: I have finished the work which thou gavest me to do. And now, O Father, glorify thou me with thine own self with the glory which I had with thee before the world was." John 17:4-5

"And they glorified God in me." Galatians 1:24

GOD: "And God spake all these words, saying, I am the LORD thy God, which have brought thee out of the land of Egypt, out of the house of bondage. Thou shalt have no other gods before me." Exodus 20: 1-3

"God is not a man, that he should lie; neither the son of man, that he should repent: hath he said, and shall he not do it? or hath he spoken, and shall he not make it good?" Numbers 23:19

"And the children of Reuben and the children of Gad called the altar Ed: for it shall be a witness between us that the LORD is God." Joshua 22:34

"And also the Strength of Israel will not lie or repent: for he is not a man, that he should repent." 1 Samuel 15:29

73

"Fear ye not, neither be afraid: have not I told thee from that time, and have declared it? ye are even my witnesses. Is there a God beside me? yea, there is no God; I know not any." Isaiah 44:8

"And without controversy great is the mystery of godliness: God was manifest in the flesh, justified in the Spirit, seen of angels, preached unto the Gentiles, believed on in the world, received up in glory." 1 Timothy 3:16

Plug in

Our Heavenly Father, we are thankful that you are God;
the one and only true Living God; The Awesome God.
You are the all-seeing, all-knowing, and all-powerful God.
We thank you there is no God besides you.
There is none other to seek for; there is none that exist.
You are the only God that does what He says, and says what He does.

You are God and not man, that you should lie.
The Scriptures tell us You came down to earth,
and were received UP again in glory.
Thank you for coming that we might rise up in salvation.
You were made known in the flesh,
and justified in the Spirit. You were seen of angels,
and believed on in the world.
It was You — born of a virgin, wrapped in flesh,
laid in a manger, died and rose again.
A mystery, yes indeed!
But by faith, this we believe.

I have no doubt Jesus is God; it was Him
before the foundation of the world.
God, the only God, we say, "thank you."

GOOD: "O taste and see that the LORD is good; blessed is the man that trusteth in him." Psalm 34:8

"O give thanks unto the LORD, for he is good: for his mercy endureth for ever." Psalm 107:1

"Oh that men would praise the LORD for his goodness, and for this wonderful works to the children of men!" Psalm 107: 8, 15, 21, 31.

"The LORD is good to all: and his tender mercies are over all his works." Psalm 145:9

"How God anointed Jesus of Nazareth with the Holy Ghost and with power: who went about doing good, and healing all that were oppressed of the devil; for God was with him." Acts 10:38

Plug in

God is good! Oh, so good!
We thank and give you praise.
We praise you for your goodness and your wonderful works!
We are thankful that your goodness and your mercy
shall follow us all the days of our lives.
No matter how bad things sometime seem to be,
you are always all Good.
Teach us to know we can never be without good,
because we're never without you.
Lord, thank you for abiding in us that we may
display your goodness throughout the world.

No matter how bad things seem to be, God has never been bad to me;
He has always been good, and still is.
God, the Good God, we say, "thank you."

GREAT: "Great is the LORD, and greatly to be praised in the city of our God, in the mountain of his holiness." Psalm 48:1

"For the LORD is a great God, and a great King above all gods." Psalm 95:3

"For the LORD is great, and greatly to be praised: he is to be feared above all gods." Psalm 96:4

"Great is the LORD, and greatly to be praised; and his greatness is unsearchable." Psalm 145:3

GUIDE, *Our:* "I will instruct thee and teach thee in the way which thou shalt go. I will guide thee with mine eye." Psalm 32:8

"For this God is our God for ever and ever: he will be our guide even unto death." Psalm 48:14

"I will go before thee, and make the crooked places straight: I will break in pieces the gates of brass, and cut in sunder the bars of iron:" Isaiah 45:2

"Wilt thou not from this time cry unto me, My father, thou art the guide of my youth?" Jeremiah 3:4

Plug in

I thank and praise God because He is my:

A_____

B_____

C_____

D_____

E_____

F_____

G_____

Chapter 2

THANKING and PRAISING GOD for GOD through H, I, J, K

H

HAPPINESS, *Our:* "Happy is that people, that is in such a case: yea, happy is that people, whose God is the LORD." Psalm 144:15

"Happy is he that hath the God of Jacob for his help, whose hope is in the LORD his God:" Psalm 146:5

"He that handleth a matter wisely shall find good: and whoso trusteth in the LORD, happy is he." Proverbs 16:20

Plug in

Would you agree we all want to be happy?
For what is money, if we're not happy?
What is fame, if it leaves us empty?
What is having a big house, if every corner is misery?
What is having a big car,
if it leaves one wondering which way to go?
Why not trust God with our money?
Trust Him with our fame. Sanctify our house to Him.
Trust Him with our car. Let Him take the wheel and steer us
the way He wants to go.
By doing this, we will see true happiness only lies in God.

God in my heart produces happiness in my life.
God, our Happiness, we say, "thank you."

HEALER, *Our*: "And said, If thou wilt diligently hearken to the voice of the LORD thy God, and wilt do that which is right in his sight, and wilt give ear to his commandments, and keep all his statutes, I will put none of these diseases upon thee, which I have brought upon the Egyptians: for I am the LORD that healeth thee." Exodus 15:26

"If my people, which are called by my name, shall humble themselves, and pray, and seek my face, and turn from their wicked ways; then will I hear from heaven, and will forgive their sin, and will heal their land." 2 Chronicles 7:14

"He sent his word, and healed them, and delivered them from their destructions." Psalm 107:20

"He healeth the broken in heart, and bindeth up their wounds." Psalm 147:3

"Who his own self bare our sins in his own body on the tree, that we, being dead to sins, should live unto righteousness; by whose stripes ye were healed." 1 Peter 2:24

HEART FIXER, *Our*: "And all the kings of the earth sought the presence of Solomon, to hear his wisdom, that God had put in his heart." 2 Chronicles 9:23

"Create in me a clean heart, O God; and renew a right spirit within me." Psalm 51:10

"And they shall be my people, and I will be their God: And I will give them one heart, and one way, that they may fear me for ever, for the good of them, and of their children after them:" Jeremiah 32:38-39

"And put no difference between us and them, purifying their hearts by faith." Acts 15:9

Plug in

Lord, we thank and praise you for being our Heart Fixer.
Sometimes our heart can be in terrible shape.
It may need more than a physical fixing.
It might need a spiritual healing.
Thank you for being the only One who can fix a spiritually sick heart.
Fix our heart that we may know
how to handle a matter wisely.
Create in us a clean heart and renew a right spirit within us.
With you as our spiritual heart surgeon, then and only then
we can declare with thanksgiving:
"My heart is fixed, O God, my heart is fixed;
I will sing and give praise."

Thanking God in all things keeps my heart thriving.
God, our Heart Fixer, we say, "thank you."

HELPER, *Our:* "But I am poor and needy; yet the Lord thinketh upon me: thou art my help and my deliverer; make no tarrying, O my God." Psalm 40:17

"Give us help from trouble: for vain is the help of man." Psalm 60:11.

"Help us, O God of our salvation, for the glory of thy name: and deliver us, and purge away our sins, for thy name's sake." Psalm 79:9

"Unless the LORD had been my help, my soul had almost dwelt in silence." Psalm 94:17

"So that we may boldly say, The Lord is my helper, and I will not fear what man shall do unto me." Hebrews 13:6

HOLY: "Exalt ye the LORD our God, and worship at his footstool; for he is holy." Psalm 99:5

"He sent redemption unto his people: He hath commanded his covenant forever: holy and reverend is his name." Psalm 111:9

"For He that is mighty hath done to me great things; and holy is his name." Luke 1:49

"And to the angel of the church in Philadelphia write, These things saith he that is holy, he that is true, he that hath the key of David, he that openeth, and no man shutteth; and shutteth, and no man openeth;" Revelation 3:7

"And the four beasts had each of them six wings about him; and they were full of eyes within: and they rest not day and night, saying, Holy, holy, holy, Lord God Almighty, which was, and is, and is to come." Revelation 4:8

Plug in

To know God is to know, He is Holy.
He doesn't sin, never has sinned,
never will sin, and cannot sin.
We're the ones who were once lost in sin,
in need of a sinless Savior.
God sent His Son, Jesus Christ our Lord, to pay our sinful debt.
Now we can be partakers of His holiness and know
Him for who He is, and what He has done.
He is Holy and did take on sin for us.

Holy, holy, holy is the Lord God Almighty, and
sin can't touch that.
God, the Holy God, we say, "thank you."

HOLY SPIRIT, *The:* "Now the birth of Jesus Christ was on this wise: When as his mother Mary was espoused to Joseph, before they came together, she was found with child of the Holy Ghost." Matthew 1:18

"God is a Spirit: and they that worship him must worship him in spirit and in truth." John 4:24

"Even the Spirit of truth; whom the world cannot receive, because it seeth him not, neither knowest him; but ye know him; for he dwellest with you, and shall be in you." John 14:17

"Now the Lord is that Spirit: and where the Spirit of the Lord is, there is liberty." 2 Corinthians 3:17

"For there are three that bear record in heaven, the Father, the Word, and the Holy Ghost: and these three are one." 1 John: 5:7

HOPE, *Our:* "And now, Lord, what wait I for? my hope is in thee." Psalm 39:7

"Why art thou cast down, O my soul? And why art thou disquieted in me? hope thou in God: for I shall yet praise him for the help of his countenance." Psalm 42:5

"Be not a terror unto me: thou art my hope in the day of evil." Jeremiah 17:17

"Now the God of hope fill you with all joy and peace in believing, that ye may abound in hope, through the power of the Holy Ghost." Romans 15:13

"To whom God would make known what is the riches of the glory of this mystery among the Gentiles; which is Christ in you, the hope of glory:" Colossians 1:27

Plug in

Father, we thank and praise you for giving us hope.
Help us to look to you, long for you, and hold on to you.
Hope in you fills us with joy and peace in believing
we will see a brighter day, despite these turbulent times.
Hope in you relaxes our mind.
Hope in you helps us to lie down at night with sweet sleep.
Hope in you provides comfort to get up and start again.
You are our only hope.

When I felt hopeless, God gave me hope; I hope in Him.
God, our Hope, we say, "thank you."

HOSANNA: "And the multitudes that went before, and that followed, cried, saying, Hosanna to the Son of David. Blessed is he that cometh in the name of the Lord; Hosanna in the highest." Matthew 21:9

"And they that went before, and they that followed, cried, saying, Hosanna; Blessed is he that cometh in the name of the Lord:" Mark 11:9

"Took branches of palm trees and went forth to meet him, and cried, Hosanna: Blessed is the King of Israel that cometh in the name of the Lord." John 12:13

HOUSEHOLDER, *Our*: "For the kingdom of heaven is like unto a man that is an householder, which went out early in the morning to hire labours into his vineyard." Matthew 20:1

"As we have therefore opportunity, let us do good unto all men, especially unto them who are of the household of faith." Galatians 6:10

"Now therefore ye are no more strangers and foreigners, but fellowcitizens with the saints, and of the household of God;" Ephesians 2:19

Plug in

*Father God, we are thankful those who have accepted Jesus as Savior
are members of your household;
and what a unique household it is!
It is a place where people are born again,
loving each other; using opportunities to do
good to everyone, especially those who share the house.*

*We praise you for making us family, and Jesus the head of the house.
We thank you, He's the bread winner, supplier, keeper,
and the provider. It is said in your Word,
you will supply our every need
according to your riches in glory by Christ Jesus.
In this we are totally dependent on you.
We need only submit in faith, ourselves, our dwelling,
and everything in our dwelling to your care.
Since we are members of this great household of faith,
help us to do unto others as you have done unto us.*

**I am no visitor or stranger in God's house; I've been born
into the family.**
God, our Householder, we say, "thank you."

I

I AM, *The*: "And God said unto Moses, I AM THAT I AM: and he said, Thus shalt thou say unto the children of Israel, I AM hath sent me unto you." Exodus 3:14

"Jesus said unto them, Verily, verily, I say unto you, Before Abraham was, I am." John 8:58

IMPARTIAL: "That ye may be the children of your Father which is in heaven: for he maketh his sun to rise on the evil and on the good, and sendeth rain on the just and on the unjust." Matthew 5:45

"But love your enemies, and do good, and lend, hoping for nothing again; and your reward shall be great, and ye shall be the children of the Highest: for he is kind unto the unthankful and to the evil." Luke 6:35

"Then Peter opened his mouth, and said, Of a truth I perceive that God is no respector of persons:" Acts 10:34

"For there is no respect of persons with God." Romans 2:11

"My brethren, have not the faith of our Lord Jesus Christ, the Lord of glory, with respect of persons." James 2:1

Plug in

Lord, we thank and praise you because we are your children,
and you love us one and all.
Thank you for raining on the just as well as the unjust;
being kind to the thankful and the unthankful.
Lord, thank you for treating us all the same,
showing no partiality.
Thank you for giving us all of your love, mercy, and grace.

Help us to love our enemies, and do good,
lending, and looking for nothing back.
Help us not to see big I and little you;
for such is not in your view.

God makes no difference in you or I, nor them or they; He's kind to all.
God, the Impartial God, we say, "thank you."

IMMANUEL: "Therefore the Lord himself shall give you a sign; Behold, a virgin shall conceive, and bear a son, and shall call his name Immanuel." Isaiah 7:14

"And he shall pass through Judah; he shall overflow and go over, he shall reach even to the neck; and the stretching out of his wings shall fill the breadth of thy land, O Immanuel." Isaiah 8:8

"Behold, a virgin shall be with child, and shall bring forth a son, and they shall call his name Emmanuel, which being interpreted is, God with us." Matthew 1:23

"Teaching them to observe all things whatsoever I have commanded you: and, lo, I am with you alway, even unto the end of the world. Amen." Matthew 28:20

IMMORTAL: "For I delivered unto you first of all that which I also received, how that Christ died for our sins according to the scriptures; And that he was buried, and that he rose again the third day according to the scriptures:" 1 Corinthians 15:3-4

"Now unto the King eternal, immortal, invisible, the only wise God, be honour and glory for ever and ever. Amen" 1 Timothy 1:17

"Who only hath immortality, dwelling in the light which no man can approach unto; whom no man hath seen, nor can see: to whom be honour and power everlasting, Amen." 1Timothy 6:16

"But is now made manifest by the appearing of our Savior Jesus Christ, who hath abolished death, and hath brought life and immortality to light through the gospel:" 2 Timothy 1:10

INCOMPARABLE: "Who is like unto thee, O LORD, among the gods? Who is like thee, glorious in holiness, fearful praises, doing wonders?" Exodus 15:11

"Wherefore thou art great, O LORD God: for there is none like thee, neither is there any God beside thee, according to all that we have heard with our ears." 2 Samuel 7:22

"Thy righteousness also, O God, is very high, who hast done great things: O God, who is like unto thee!" Psalm 71:19

"For who in the heaven can be compared unto the LORD? who among the sons of the mighty can be likened unto the LORD?" Psalm 89:6

"To whom then will ye liken God? Or what likeness will you compare unto him?" Isaiah 40:18

Plug in

Who can be compared to or be like our Lord?
And the answer is...

NO ONE. NOT ANYONE. NOBODY. NOT YOU. NOT ME.
NOT THIS. NOT THAT. NOT IT.
NOT HE. NOT SHE. NOT THEM. NOT THEY.

Nothing can be compared to our blessed Lord.

NOTHING. NOTHING IN HEAVEN. NOTHING IN EARTH.
NOTHING UNDER THE EARTH. NOTHING BEYOND.
ABSOLUTELY NOTHING!

No matter how, smart, rich, big or powerful,
No one and nothing can be compared to our Lord!
He is...

GLORIOUIS IN HOLINESS, FEARFUL IN PRAISES,
DOING WONDERS!!!

There is no one like God; He's matchless.
God, the Incomparable God, we say, "thank you."

INCREASER, *Our:* "Thou shalt increase my greatness, and comfort me on every side." Psalm 71:21

"And he increased his people greatly; and made them stronger than their enemies." Psalm 105:24

"The LORD shall increase you more and more, you and your children." Psalm 115:14

"I have planted, Apollos watered; but God gave the increase." 1 Corinthians 3:6

"But grow in the grace, and in knowledge of our Lord and Saviour Jesus Christ. To him be glory both now and for ever. Amen." 2 Peter 3:18

INFINITE: "But will God indeed dwell on the earth? behold, the heaven and heaven of heavens cannot contain thee; how much less this house that I have builded? 1 Kings 8:27

"Great is our Lord, and of great power: his understanding is infinite." Psalm 147:5

"Can any hide himself in secret places that I shall not see him? saith the LORD. Do not I fill heaven and earth? saith the LORD." Jeremiah 23:24

INITIATOR, *Our:* "Or who hath first given to him, and it shall be recompensed unto him again? For of him, and through him, and to him, are all things: to whom be glory for ever. Amen." Romans 11:35-36

"He came unto his own, and his own received him not." John 1:11

"We love him, because he first loved us." 1 John 4:19

Plug in

Father God, we thank you for taking the first step.
Before the foundation of the world you stepped out in love for us.
And what a loving God you are dear Lord!
You didn't wait for us to come to you; you came first.
You didn't wait for us to give to you; you gave first.
You didn't wait for us to receive you; you received us first.
You didn't wait for us to love you; you first loved.
You loved us so much, you didn't wait for us to make up our mind;
You just came and got us right on time.

God loving me first shows me how to love.
God, our Initiator, we say, "thank you."

INVISIBLE: "For the invisible things of him from the creation of the world are clearly seen, being understood by the things that are made, even his eternal power and Godhead; so that they are without excuse:" Romans 1:20

"In whom we have redemption though his blood, even the forgiveness of sins: Who is the image of the invisible God, the firstborn of every creature:" Colossians 1:14-15

"By faith he forsook Egypt, not fearing the wrath of the king: for he endured, as seeing him who is invisible." Hebrews 11:27

J

JEHOVAH: "Sing unto God, sing praises unto his name: extol him that rideth upon the heavens by his name JAH, and rejoice before him." Psalm 68:4

"That men may know that thou, whose name alone is JE-HO-VAH, art the most high over all the earth." Psalm 83:18

"Behold, God is my salvation; I will trust, and not be afraid: for the LORD JE-HO-VAH is my strength and my song; he also is become my salvation." Isaiah 12:2

JESUS: "If ye had known me, ye should have known my Father also: and from henceforth ye know him, and have seen him." John 14:7

"Jesus saith unto him, Have I been so long time with you, and yet hast thou not known me, Philip? he that hath seen me hath seen the Father; and how sayest thou then, Shew us the Father? John 14:9

"Believe me that I am in the Father, and the Father in me: or else believe me for the very works' sake." John 14:11

"And I answered, Who art thou, Lord? And he said unto me, I am JESUS of Nazareth, whom thou persecutest." Acts 22:8

Plug in

Jesus, Jesus, Jesus; wonderful Jesus, our Savior;
who loved us so much and gave Himself for the world.
Jesus, Jesus, Jesus; wonderful Jesus, God our Savior;
who suffered and died, yet rose again, and is coming back for us!
Jesus, Jesus, Jesus; wonderful Jesus, our Savior!

Let's go tell it on the mountains; shout through the hills and valleys;
lift our hands both day and night that Jesus Christ our Lord, our Life,
our Perfect Sacrifice, our Shining Light, is the Savior.

You're worthy, so worthy of our praise;
for us, dear Lord, you came to save.
Jesus, Jesus, Jesus, wonderful Jesus!

God has saved me, is saving me,
and will save me eternally.
Jesus, our God, we say, "thank you."

JOY OF OUR SALVATION, *The:* "Then said he unto them, Go your way, eat the fat, and drink the sweet, and send portions unto them for whom nothing is prepared: for this day is holy unto our Lord: neither be ye sorry; for the joy of the LORD is your strength." Nehemiah 8:10

"Restore unto me the joy of thy salvation; and uphold me with thy free spirit." Psalm 51:12

"These things have I spoken unto you, that my joy might remain in you, and that your joy might be full." John 15:11

"And ye now therefore have sorrow: but I will see you again, and your heart shall rejoice, and your joy no man taketh from you." John 16:22

Plug in

Dear God, we're thankful no man can take away our joy.
Our joy is rooted and grounded in you.
When we go through trials, joy in you keeps us strong.

Weeping may endure for the night, but joy comes with the morning light.
Your joy remains in the rain or shine; never changing, the
same every time.
We don't understand nor can we explain how your joy keeps us sane!

Here we are, lifting holy hands to you;
The Joy of Our Salvation, which carries us through.
Thank you for giving permanent joy that provides strength to press on
Until we come rejoicing to our permanent home.

In my lowest hours, the joy of the Lord strengthened me.
God, the Joy Of Our Salvation, we say, "thank you."

JUDGE, *The*: "And he shall judge the world in righteousness, he shall minister judgment to the people in uprightness." Psalm 9:8

"And the heavens shall declare his righteousness: for God is judge himself. Se-lah," Psalm 50:6

"O let the nations be glad and sing for joy: for thou shall judge the people righteously, and govern the nations upon the earth. Selah." Psalm 67:4

"For the LORD is our judge, the LORD is our Lawgiver, the LORD is our King; he will save us." Isaiah 33:22

"I CHARGE thee therefore before God, and the Lord Jesus Christ, who shall judge the quick and the dead, at his appearing and his kingdom;" 2 Timothy 4:1

JUSTIFIER, *The:* "For all have sinned, and come short of the glory of God; Being justified freely by his grace through the redemption that is in Christ Jesus:" Romans 3:23-24

"To declare, I say, at this time his righteousness: that he might be just, and the justifier of him which believeth in Jesus." Romans 3:26

"Therefore being justified by faith, we have peace with God through our Lord Jesus Christ." Romans 5:1

K

KEEPER, *Our:* "For he shall give his angels charge over thee, to keep thee in all thy ways." Psalm 91:11

"The LORD is thy keeper: the LORD is thy shade upon thy right hand." Psalm 121:5

"Set a watch, O LORD, before my mouth; keep the door of my lips." Psalm 141:3

"Keep me from the snares which they have laid for me, and the gins of the workers of iniquity." Psalm 141:9

Plug in

We are thankful God is our Keeper.
He keeps us from the traps of the enemy, and those who work against us.
We have no ability to keep ourselves; we may try,
but it is God doing the keeping.
He is the shade upon our right hand.
He keeps us from scorching in the burning heat of life.
Whatever our shade may be,
it is God giving the comfort and the relief.
Why not get out of the hot weather,
and get under His protective shade?

No matter how hot I get, God keeps me cool in the heat of the day.
God, our Keeper, we say, "thank you."

KING, *The*: "Lift up your heads, O ye gates; and be ye lift up, ye everlasting doors; and the King of glory shall come in. Who is this King of glory? The LORD strong and mighty, the LORD mighty in battle." Psalm 24:7-8

"For God is the King of all the earth; sing ye praises with understanding." Psalm 47:7:

"Then said I, Woe is me! For I am undone; because I am a man of unclean lips, and I dwell in the midst of a people of unclean lips: for mine eyes have seen the King, the LORD of Hosts." Isaiah 6:5

"I am the LORD, your Holy one, the creator of Israel, your King." Isaiah 43:15

"And he hath on his vesture and on his thigh a name written, KING OF KINGS, AND LORD OF LORDS." Revelation 19:16

Plug in

Have you seen the King, the Lord of Hosts?
Oh, how magnificent to behold Him!
Oh, how wonderful to express gratitude to Him and for Him,
His Majesty; to bow to Him in His glory!
As wretched and undone as we are; people with unclean lips,
living among those of unclean lips; yet, to see the King
is truly an amazing thing!
Let's shout and give glory to our King;
The Lord of Hosts, the King of Kings, and Lord of Lords!

When I saw the King, I bowed.
God, our King, we say, "thank you."

Plug In

I thank and praise God because He is my:

H_____

I_____

J_____

K_____

Chapter 3

THANKING and PRAISING GOD for GOD through L, M, N, O, P

L

LEADER, *Our:* "So the LORD alone did lead him, and there was no strange god with him." Deuteronomy 32:12

"Lead me, O LORD, in thy righteousness because of mine enemies; make thy way straight before my face." Psalm 5:8

"He maketh me to lie down in green pastures: he leadeth me beside the still waters." Psalm 23:2

"Thou leddest thy people like a flock by the hand of Moses and Aaron." Psalm 77:20

"to him the porter openeth; and the sheep hear his voice: and he calleth his own sheep by name, and leadeth them out. And when he putteth forth his own sheep, he goeth before them, and the sheep follow him: for they know his voice." John 10:3

Plug in

We've heard the saying, let the Lord lead you.
Yes, we must let the Lord lead. Know that He's not going to force
His leadership upon us. He wants to lead and make our paths straight.
Why not give Him the reins of our hearts and follow Him?

We need the Lord as our leader because we have an enemy;
an enemy that wants to lead us into everything that's against our Lord.
It pays to follow the Lord's leadership. He will lead us into
His righteousness, and will make our way straight right before our eyes.

When I follow God's lead, I don't have to wonder
which way to go.
God, our Leader, we say, "thank you."

LIFE, *Our:* "And the LORD God formed man of the dust of the ground, and breathed into his nostrils the breath of life; and man became a living soul." Genesis 2:7

"In him was life; and the life was the light of men." John 1:4

"For in him we live, and move, and have our being; as certain also of your own poets have said, For we are also his offspring." Acts 17:28

"For me to live is Christ, and to die is gain." Philippians 1:21

"When Christ, who is our life, shall appear, then shall ye also appear with him in glory." Colossians 3:4

LIFTER, *Our:* "But thou, O LORD, art a shield for me; my glory, and the lifter up of mine head." Psalm 3:3

"Have mercy upon me, O LORD; consider my trouble which I suffer of them that hate me, thou that liftest me up from the gates of death:" Psalm 9:13

"Humble yourselves in the sight of the Lord, and he shall lift you up." James 4:10

Plug in

Dear Lord, it is you who lifts us up. We are grateful.
We thank you for enabling us to rise from the challenges of life
that tend to press us down.
You are the lifter of our head.
We thank you for lifting us out of "the stuff" we used to wallow in.
We thank you for showing us that pride is not the way up;
it will surely bring us down.
We thank you for showing us that by
humbling ourselves in your sight is what pleases you.
Help us to humble ourselves and get rid of high-mindedness.
Oh Lord, we lift our hands in thanksgiving and praise to you.

God lifted me by bringing me down in humility.
God, our Lifter, we say, "thank you."

LIGHT, *The*: "The LORD is my light and my salvation; whom shall I fear? The LORD is the strength of my life; of whom shall I be afraid." Psalm 27:1

"And the light shineth in darkness; and the darkness comprehended it not." John 1:5

"Then spake Jesus again unto them, saying, I am the light of the world: he that followeth me shall not walk in darkness, but shall have the light of life." John 8:12

"As long as I am in the world, I am the light of the world." John 9:5

"I am come a light into the world, that whosoever believeth on me should not abide in darkness." John 12:46

"This then is the message which we have heard of him, and declare unto you, that God is light, and in him is no darkness at all." 1 John 1:5

LORD, *The:* "Know ye that the LORD he is God; it is he that hath made us, and not we ourselves; we are his people, and the sheep of his pasture." Psalm 100:3

"God is the LORD, which hath shewed us light: bind the sacrifice with cords, even unto the horns of the altar." Psalm 118:27

"I am the LORD: that is my name: and my glory will I not give to another, neither my praise to graven images." Isaiah 42:8

"But let him that glorieth, glory in this, that he understandeth and knoweth me, that I am the LORD which exercise lovingkindness, judgment, and righteousness, in the earth: for in these things I delight, said the LORD." Jeremiah 9:24

"Therefore let all the house of Isreal know assuredly, that God hath made that same Jesus, whom you have crucified, both Lord and Christ." Acts 2:36

"One Lord, one faith, one baptism," Ephesians 4:5

LOVE: "The LORD hath appeared of old unto me, saying, Yea, I have loved thee with an everlasting love: therefore with lovingkindness have I drawn thee." Jeremiah 31:3

"Beloved, let us love one another: for love is of God; and every one that loveth is born of God, and knoweth God." 1 John 4:7

"He that loveth not knoweth not God; for God is love." 1 John 4:8

Plug in

*God of Love, we thank and praise you for your love toward us.
You loved us so much that you gave Love to the whole world
in the person of Jesus Christ our Lord;
the perfect, sacrificial, impartial, and patient kind of love.
Thank you that your love is to all and for all.
It embraces the young and the old, the rich and the poor,
the learned and the unlearned,
the hard to love, loveless, and the love deprived.*

*Dear Lord, help us to be reflectors of you
by loving who and what you love.
We realize we couldn't do anything to make you love us;
you just did.
We're thankful that everyone can have this sweet and great love;
redeeming and raising love; and this saving and everlasting love.*

**I thank God for loving me unconditionally; He is my
All-time Lover.**
God, our Love, we say, "thank you."

M

MAJESTIC: "Gird thy sword upon thy thigh, O most mighty, with thy glory and thy majesty. And in thy majesty ride prosperously because of truth and meekness and righteousness; and thy right hand shall teach thee terrible things." Psalm 45:3-4

"The LORD reigneth, he is clothed with majesty, the LORD is clothed with strength wherewith he hath girded himself; the world also is stablished, that it cannot be moved." Psalm 93:1

"I will speak of the glorious honour of thy majesty, and of thy wondrous works." Psalm 145:5

"For we have not followed cunningly devised fables, when we made known unto you the power and coming of our Lord Jesus Christ, but were eyewitnesses of his majesty." 2 Peter 1:16

MAKER, *The:* "And God said, Let us make man in our image, after our likeness: and let them have dominion over the fish of the sea, and over the fowl of the air, and over the cattle, and over all the earth, and over every creeping thing that creepeth upon the earth." Genesis 1:26

"O come, let us worship and bow down: let us kneel before the LORD our maker." Psalm 95:6

"The rich and the poor meet together: The LORD is the maker of them all." Proverbs 22:2

"Thus said the LORD, thy redeemer, and he that formed thee from the womb, I am the LORD that maketh all things, that stretcheth forth the heavens alone; that spreadeth abroad the earth by myself;" Isaiah 44:24

"And he that sat upon the throne said, Behold, I make all things new. And he said unto me, Write: for these words are true and faithful." Revelation 21:5

Plug in

Look at God our Maker! The Lord our Redeemer!
He that formed us from the womb.
He made the world, man, and everything in the world.
He alone stretched forth the heavens. He made it all by Himself.
He didn't need any constructional, architectural,
electrical, or oceanographic advice;
He followed His own perfect design.
We are thankful nothing exploded from a dark hole,
and caused the world, you, or I into existence;
it was God.

God made it all. He did it His way; the darkness for the night,
and the light for the day.
God, our Maker, we say, "thank you."

MASTER: "Then Jesus turned, and saw them following, and saith unto them, What seek ye? They said unto him, Rabbi, (which is to say, being interpreted, Master,) where dwellest thou? John 1:38

"And his disciples asked him, saying, Master, who did sin, this man, or his parents, that he was born blind?" John 9:2

"Ye call me Master and Lord: and ye say well; for so I am. If I then, your Lord and Master, have washed your feet; ye also ought to wash one another's feet." John 13:13-14

MERCIFUL: "(For the LORD thy God is a merciful God;) he will not forsake thee, neither destroy thee, nor forget the covenant of thy fathers which he sware unto them." Deuteronomy 4:31

"I will be glad and rejoice in thy mercy: for thou hast considered my trouble; thou has known my soul in adversities." Psalm 31:7

"Let thy mercy, O LORD, be upon us, according as we hope in thee." Psalm 33:22

"The LORD is merciful and gracious, slow to anger, and plenteous in mercy." Psalm 103:8

Plug in

God of Mercy, how can we say thanks for your kindness toward us?
We thank you for not giving us what we deserve.
Lord, although we mess up every day,
and miss the mark in some form in some way;
we thank you for not dealing with us according to our mess.
We thank you for giving us of your mercy.
Undeserving that we are,
you have poured your vial of mercy on us.

Because of God's mercy, I'm still here.
God, the Merciful, we say, "thank you."

MESSIAH, *The:* "He first findeth his own brother Simon, and saith unto him, We have found the Mes-si-as, which is, being interpreted, the Christ." John 1:41

"The woman saith unto him, I know that Mes-si-as cometh, which is called Christ: when he is come, he will tell us all things. Jesus saith unto her, I that speak unto thee am he." John 4:25-26

MIND RESTORER, *Our:* "Thou wilt keep him I perfect peace, whose mind is stayed on thee: because he trustedth in thee." Isaiah 26:3

"Then they went out to see what was done; and came to Jesus, and found the man, out of whom the devils were departed, sitting at the feet of Jesus, clothed and in his right mind; and they were afraid." Luke 8:35

"Let this mind be in you, which was also in Christ Jesus." Philippians 2:5

Plug in

Father God, we thank and praise you our Mind Restorer.
We bless your name for restoring us in the right frame of mind.
According to Luke 8:35,
after meeting Jesus, this man changed.
He was no longer the same.
His thinking, behavior, and position changed.
He's no longer possessed with a disturb mind.
He's no longer cutting himself.
He's no longer running to and fro.
He's no longer living among the dead.
He's at peace, sitting at the feet of Jesus.
That man is now approachable, and in the right position
to stop the devil from controlling his mind.

If we want the devil to stop confusing and controlling our mind
we also must sit at the feet of Jesus.
At His feet there is peace, calmness, and clarity of thought.
Like this man, we too must position ourselves
before Him in order to break the enemy's control over us?

I would have literally lost my mind, if I hadn't sat at Jesus's feet.
God, our Mind Restorer, we say, "thank you."

MULTIPLIER, *Our:* "And I will make thy seed to multiply as the stars of heaven, and will give unto thy seed all these countries; and in thy seed shall all the nation of the earth be blessed; Because that Abraham obeyed my voice, and kept my charge, my commandments, my statutes, and my laws." Genesis 26:4-5

"Saying, Surely blessing I will bless thee, and multiplying I will multiply thee." Hebrews 6:14

N

NEVER-ENDING: "Behold, God is great, and we know him not, neither can the number of his years be searched out." Job 36:26

"But the LORD shall endure for ever: he hath prepared his throne for judgment." Psalm 9:7

"Before the mountains were brought forth, or ever thou hadst formed the earth and the world, even from everlasting to everlasting, thou art God" Psalm 90:2

"But thou are the same, and thy years shall have no end." Psalm 102:27

"Thy kingdom is an everlasting kingdom, and thy dominion endures throughout all generations." Psalm 145:13

Plug in

*Father God, we thank and praise
you because you are God without beginning or ending.
You always were, is, and will forever be.
Knowing this gives us the assurance
you've always been there for us and always will.
Thank you for never leaving us alone.
Thank you for being there in the daytime,
night time, light time, dark time, and stormy time.
Thank you for always seeing us through.
You've not only been in the past; you will also be in the future.*

My God will never end; He's endless.
God, the Never-ending God, we say "thank you."

NOW GOD, *The:* "God is our refuge and strength, a very present help in trouble." Psalm 46:1

"The LORD is nigh unto all them that call upon him, to all that call upon him in truth." Psalm 145:18

"Am I a God at hand, saith the LORD and not a God afar off?" Jeremiah 23:23

"And he said unto Jesus, Lord, remember me when thou comest unto thy kingdom. And Jesus said unto him, Verily I say unto thee, To day shalt thou be with me in paradise." Luke 23:42-43

"Wherefore (as the Holy Ghost saith, To day if ye will hear his voice, Harden not your hearts, as in the provocation, in the day of temptation in the wilderness:" Hebrews 3:7

O

OMNIPOTENT: *(All Powerful):* "God hath spoken once; twice have I heard this; that power belongeth unto God." Psalm 62:11

"Behold, I am the LORD, the God of all flesh; is there any thing too hard for me?" Jeremiah 32:27

"And Jesus came and spake unto them, saying, all power is given unto me in heaven and in earth." Matthew 28:18

"Let every soul be subject unto the higher powers. For there is no power but of God: the powers that be are ordained of God." Romans 13:1

"Now to him that is of power to stablish you according to my gospel, and the preaching of Jesus Christ, according to the revelation of the mystery, which was kept secret since the world began," Romans 16:25

"And I heard as it were the voice of a great multitude, and as the voice of many waters, and as the voice of mighty thunderings saying, Alleluia: for the Lord God Omnipotent reigneth." Revelation 19:6

Plug in

Father, we thank you, the Omnipotent, all Powerful God.
You have the absolute, reigning, and controlling power.
All power is subject to you and will forever be.
May we all be thankful and declare:
"Ah Lord GOD! Behold, thou hast made the heaven and the earth by thy great power and stretched out arm, and there is nothing too hard for thee."

With your power you can do anything you please.
You alone are well able and capable to perform whatever the task may be.

Let's not lose heart regarding any matter;
The Lord God Omnipotent reigns!
Let's not focus on the thing that seems so difficult;
The Lord God Omnipotent reigns!
or the bad things we think could happen;
The Lord God Omnipotent reigns!
Let's be thankful we have the all-powerful God,
who continues to surround with His amazing power.

God is my all-power source; I'm surrounded.
God, the Omnipotent God, we say, "thank you."

OMNIPRESENT (*Present everywhere*): "Whither shall I go from thy spirit? Or whither shall I flee from thy presence? If I ascend up into heaven, thou art there: if I make my bed in hell, behold, thou art there. If I take the wings of the morning, and dwell in the uttermost parts of the sea; Even there shall thy hand lead me, and thy right hand shall hold me." Psalm 139: 7-10

"That they should seek the Lord, if haply they might feel after him, and find him, though he be not far from every one of us:" Acts 17:27

Plug in

Isn't it great to be assured, there is no place
we can go where God is not?
No, not one place. Even if we made our beds in hell,
He's there.
In every direction, God is there.
In every dimension of sight and sound,
He's there.

In any place He can be found.
In the mountains so high and the valley so deep,
He's there.
In the oceans so vast and rivers so wide,
He's there.
In the earth below and the heavens above,
He's there.
Beyond our sight, He's there.
Beyond our hearing,
He's there.
Beyond our very imagination,
God is right there.

Father, all praises and thanksgiving be to your name.
Everyone and everything is exposed before you.
You're everywhere all the time, and all the time you're everywhere.

With God, I can never be all by myself;
I have ever-present company.
God, the Omnipresent God, we say, "thank you."

OMNISCIENT (*All Knowing*): "For the LORD knoweth the way of the righteous: but the way of the ungodly shall perish." Psalm 1:6

"O LORD, thou hast searched me, and known me. Thou knowest my downsitting and mine uprising, thou understandest my thought afar off. Thou compassest my path and my lying down, and art aquainted with all my ways. For there is not a word in my tongue, but, lo, O LORD, thou knoweth it all together." Psalm 139:1-4

"For I know their works and their thoughts: it shall come, that I will gather all nations and tongues; and they shall come, and see my glory." Isaiah 66:18

"Be not ye therefore like unto them; for your Father knoweth what things ye have need of, before you ask him." Matthew 6:8

"Come, see a man, which told me all things that I ever did: is not this the Christ?" John 4:29

"The Lord knoweth how to deliver the godly out of temptations, and to reserve the unjust unto the day of judgment to be punished." 2 Peter 2:9

Plug in

Father God, we offer thanksgiving to you the Omniscient,
all-knowing God.
Simply and profoundly put, you know everybody and everything.
You know the way of the righteous, and the way of ungodly.
No one and nothing gets passed you. There is not a
word we can say
or think that's hidden from you. You know it all.
You know what we need before we ask. You know our very thoughts.
You are aware when we sit down and rise up. You are familiar with
everything about us. Thank you Lord, there is not a situation we
can encounter that you are not aware of;
you know all the temptations we face.
There is no need to try to tell you how to handle any situation.
No need to tell you how to handle your people or do your job.
We are thankful you are aware of the ins, outs, ups,
downs, over, under, and in between.
You know all, and all you know.
We are thankful, Lord, we have no need to worry because
you already know.
You know what's going on beforehand, on hand, and out of hand.

I don't have to tell God what's going on; He already knows.
God, the Omniscient God, we say, "thank you."

130

OPENER OF IRON GATES, *The:* "When they were past the first and second ward, they came unto the iron gate that leadeth unto the city; which opened to them of his own accord: and they went out, and passed on through one street; and forthwith the angel departed from him." Acts 12:10

OVERCOMER OF THE WORLD, *The:* "These things I have spoken unto you, that in me ye might have peace. In the world ye shall have tribulation: but be of good cheer; I have overcome the world." John 16:33

"Ye are of God, little children, and have overcome them: because greater is he that is in you, than he that is in the world." I John 4:4

OWNER, *The:* "Behold, the heaven and the heaven of heavens is the LORD's thy God, the earth also, with all that therein is." Deuteronomy 10:14

"The earth is the LORD's, and the fullness thereof; the world, and they that dwell therein. For he hath founded it upon the seas, and established it upon the floods." Psalm 24:1-2

"For every beast of the forest is mine, and the cattle upon a thousand hills. I know all the fowls of the mountains: and the wild beasts of the field are mine. If I were hungry, I would not tell thee: for the world is mine, and the fullness thereof." Psalm 50:10-12

"For you are bought with a price: therefore glorify God in your body, and in your spirit, which are God's." 1 Corinthians 6:20

P

PEACE, *Our*: "And the LORD said unto him, Peace be unto thee; fear not: thou shalt not die. Then Gideon built an altar there unto the LORD, and called it Jehovah Shalom: unto this day it is yet in Ophrah of the Abiezrites." Judges 6:23-24

"For unto us a child is born, unto us a son is given: and the government shall be upon his shoulder: and his name shall be called Wonderful, Counsellor, The mighty God, The everlasting Father, The Prince of Peace." Isaiah 9:6

"Peace I leave with you, my peace I give unto you: not as the world giveth, give I unto you. Let not your heart be troubled, neither let it be afraid." John 14:27

"For God is not the author of confusion, but of peace, as in all churches of the saints." 1 Corinthians 14:33

"Now the Lord of peace himself give you peace always by all means. The Lord be with you all." 2 Thessalonians 3:16

Plug in

What a blessing of peace the Lord Himself gives!
God made peace available through Christ Jesus our Lord.
Lord, we thank you. We couldn't buy it; we couldn't borrow it.
Peace isn't for sale; peace was given.

Troubled hearts, be no more.
Anxiety, out the door.
Confusion, be gone.
God has given us peace through our journey home.

The peace of God keeps me calm and free from alarm.
God, our Peace, we say, "thank you."

PERFECT: "As for God, his way is perfect: the word of the LORD is tried: he is a buckler to all those that trust in him." Psalm 18:30

"Out of Zion, the perfection of beauty, God hath shinned." Psalm 50:2

"Be ye therefore perfect, even as your father which is in heaven is perfect." Matthew 5:48

"But Christ being come an high priest of good things to come, by a greater and more perfect tabernacle, not made with hands, this is to say, not of this building;" Hebrews 9:11

Plug in

Father God, we thank you because you alone are perfect.
You have fulfilled the demand of a perfect lamb slain
before the foundation of the world.
We are thankful there is no err, stain, or spot in you.
You are perfect in everything you say and do.

You are perfect in your beauty, which surrounds us.
You are perfect in your counsel, which instructs us.
You are perfect in your grace, which keeps us.
You are perfect in your discipline, which teaches us.
You are perfect in your
way, will, and Word.

Everything in and about God is perfection.
God, the Perfect One, we say, "thank you."

POSSESSER, *Our:* "And Abram said to the king of Sodom, I have lifted up mine hand unto the LORD, the most high God, the possessor of heaven and earth." Genesis 14:22

"For thou hast possessed my reins: thou has covered me in my mother's womb." Psalm 139:13

"The LORD possessed me in the beginning of his way, before his works of old." Proverbs 8:22

POTTER, *Our:* "Oh house of Israel, cannot I do with you as this potter? saith the LORD Behold, as the clay is in the potter's hand, so are ye in mine hand, O house of Israel." Jeremiah 18:6

"Nay but, O man, who art thou that repliest against God? Shall the thing formed say to him that formed it, Why hast thou made me thus? Hath not the potter power over the clay, of the same lump to make one vessel unto honor, and another unto dishonor." Romans 9:20-21

PRAYER ANSWERER, *Our:* "My voice shalt thou hear in the morning, O LORD; in the morning will I direct my prayer unto thee, and will look up." Psalm 5:3

"The LORD hath heard my supplication; the LORD will receive my prayer." Psalm 6:9

"Oh thou that hearest prayer, unto thee shall all flesh come." Psalm 65:2

"But verily God hath heard me; he hath attended to the voice of my prayer. Blessed be God, which hath not turned away my prayer, nor his mercy from me." Psalm 66:19-20

"And it shall come to pass, that before they call, I will answer; and while they are yet speaking, I will hear." Isaiah 65:24

"Ask, and it shall be given you; seek, and ye shall find; knock, and it shall be opened unto you: For every one that asketh receiveth; and he that seeketh findeth; and to him that knocketh it shall be opened." Matthew 7:7-8

"And this is the confidence that we have in him, that, if we ask anything according to his will, he heareth us:" 1 John 5:14

Plug in

Father God, we thank you because you are God who answers prayer.
We know there are some things we can answer,
but only you can answer prayer.
We can answer the door bell, telephone,
text message, emails, and the like.
Only you have the authority over answered prayer;
that's your domain.
Lord, help us to call on you, and agree in prayer.

God has all the answers I need; He's never hung up on me.
God, our Prayer Answerer, we say, "thank you."

PREDESTINATER, *The:* "For whom he did foreknow, he also did predestinate to be conformed to the image of his Son, that he might be the firstborn among many brethren. Moreover whom he did predestinate, them he also called: and whom he called, them he also justified: and whom he justified, them he also glorified." Romans 8:29-30

PREEMINENT: "Thine, O LORD, is the greatness, and the power, and the glory and the victory, and the majesty: for all that is in the heaven and in the earth is thine; thine is the kingdom, O LORD, and thou art exalted as head above all." 1 Chronicles 29:11

"But speaking the truth in love, may grow up into him in all things, which is the head, even Christ." Ephesians 4:15

"And he is the head of the body, the church: who is the beginning, the firstborn from the dead; that in all things he might have the preeminence." Colossians 1:18

"For in him dwelleth all the fullness of the Godhead bodily. And ye are complete in him, which is the head of all principality and power." Colossians 2:9-10

PRESERVER, *Our:* "Now therefore be not grieved, nor angry with yourselves, that ye sold me hither; for God did send me before you to preserve life." Genesis 45:5

"I have sinned; what shall I do unto thee, O thou preserver of men? why has thou set me as a mark against thee, so that I am a burden to myself?" Job 7:20

"Preserve me, O God: for in thee do I put my trust." Psalm 16:1

"Thou art my hiding place; thou shalt preserve me form trouble; thou shalt compass me about with songs of deliverance. Selah." Psalm 32:7

"The LORD shall preserve thee from all evil: he shall preserve thy soul. The LORD shall preserve thy going out and thy coming in from this time forth, and even forever more." Psalm 121: 7-8

Plug in

How does one thank God for His preservation power?
When we think about the word preserve, we may think
about that which is kept from danger or harm, spoilage or decay.
I'm reminded how God preserved Joseph from the evil intentions
of his brothers;
how He protected him through the pit, palace, and prison.
God not only preserved him from hurt, harm and danger,
but also with a fresh attitude of forgiveness.
Oh to be kept with such an attitude that pleases God!
No matter what we're going through God said He will keep us.
He promised to preserve our going out and coming in from this
time forth and even forever more.

I am preserved to serve by the Preserver.
God, our Preserver, we say, "thank you."

PROMOTER, *Our:* "He maketh my feet like hinds' feet, and setteth me upon my high places." Psalm 18:33

"For promotion cometh neither from the east nor from the west, nor from the south. But God is the judge: he putteth down one, and setteth up another." Psalm 75:6-7

"Because he hath set his love upon me, therefore will I deliver him: I will set him on high, because he hath known my name." Psalm 91:14

PROVIDER, *The*: "And Abraham said, My son, God will provide himself a lamb for a burnt offering: so they went both of them together." Genesis 22:8

"And Abraham called the name of that place Jehovahjireh: as it is said to this day, In the mount of the LORD it shall be seen." Genesis 22:14

"These wait all upon thee; that thou mayest give them their meat in due season. That thou givest them they gather: thou openest thine hand, they are filled with good." Psalm 104:27-28

"But my God shall supply all your need according to his riches in glory by Christ Jesus." Philippians 4:19

"God having provided some better thing for us, that they without us should not be made perfect." Hebrews 11:40

Plug In

I thank and praise God because He is my:

L _____

M _____

N _____

O _____

P _____

Chapter 4

THANKING and PRAISING GOD for GOD through Q, R, S

Q

QUALIFIER, *Our:* "Giving thanks unto the Father, which hath made us meet to be partakers of the inheritance of the saints in light:" Colossians 1:12

"If a man therefore purge himself from these, he shall be a vessel unto honour, sanctified, and meet for the master's use, and prepared unto eery good work." 2 Timothy 2:21

QUICKENER, (Giver of Life), *Our:* "My soul cleaveth unto the dust: quicken thou me according to thy word." Psalm 119:25

"(As it is written, I have made thee a father of many nations,) before him whom he believed, even God, who quickeneth the dead, and calleth those things which be not as though they were." Romans 4:17

"But if the Spirit of him that raised up Jesus from the dead dwell in you, he that raised up Christ from the dead shall also quicken your mortal bodies by his Spirit that dwelleth in you." Romans 8:11

"And you hath he quickened, who were dead in trespasses and sins;" Ephesians 2:1

QUIESCENCE, *Our:* "Teach me, and I will hold my tongue: and cause me to understand wherein I have erred." Job 6:24

"Stand in awe, and sin not: commune with your own heart upon your bed, and be still. Selah." Psalm 4:4

"Be still, and know that I am God: I will be exalted among the heathen, I will be exalted in the earth." Psalm 46:10

"He maketh the storm a calm, so that the waves thereof are still." Psalm 107:29

"But whoso hearkeneth unto me shall dwell safely, and shall be quiet from fear of evil." Proverbs 1:33

"It is good that a man should both hope and quietly wait for the salvation of the LORD." Lamentations 3:26

"And that ye study to be quiet, and to do your own business, and to work with your own hands, as we commanded you;" 1 Thessalonians 4:11

Plug in

Do you know it's God who quiets our heart?
If we can just be still.
Be still long enough to know who God is,
and what we have in Him.
If we allow God to quiet our heart, we will hear Him.

On our jobs, we sometime feel the need to still away for morning
breaks, lunch breaks, and afternoon breaks.
Why not tell ourselves,
"I'm going to take a "be-still" break with God today?"
Get alone in His company, even for a little while.
God desires to talk with me and you.
1, 2, 3, or even 15 minutes is a good start.

Having that silent uninterrupted time with God speaks volume.
He's not going to yell. Listen for His still small voice
He speaks softly. But in order to hear Him,
we must position ourselves in a manner to invite Him in.
We must get quiet.
Speak He will—if we'd be still.

When God stills my heart, I can't but hear Him.
God, our Quiescence, we say, "thank you."

145

R

RECONCILER, *The:* "To wit, that God was in Christ, reconciling the world unto himself, not imputing their trespasses unto them; and hath committed unto us the word of reconciliation." 2 Corinthians 5:19

"And, having made peace through the blood of his cross, by him to reconcile all things unto himself; by him, I say, whether they be things in earth, or things in heaven. And you, that were sometime alienated and enemies in your mind by wicked works, yet now hath he reconciled In the body of his flesh through death, to present you holy and unblameable and unreproveable in his sight." Colossians 1:20-23

Plug in

*Father God, we offer thanksgiving and praises to you.
It was you in Christ reconciling the world unto yourself.
We thank you for bridging the gap between you and man
by sending your Son, Jesus, to take on sin for us.
Thank you for restoring our relationship back to you,
making peace through the blood of His cross.
Lord, we thank you for taking away the guilt sin brings,
making it possible to talk freely with you in Jesus name.*

**I am privileged to talk to God in Jesus name
anyplace, anytime, and all the time.**
God, *our Reconciler, we say, 'thank you.'*

REDEEMER, *The:* "For I know that my redeemer liveth, and that he shall stand at the latter day upon the earth." Job 19:25

"Let the words of my mouth, and the meditation of my heart, be acceptable in thy sight, O LORD, my strength and redeemer." Psalm 19:14

"But God will redeem my soul from the power of the grave: for he shall receive me. Se-lah." Psalm. 49:15

"To redeem them that were under the law, that we might receive the adoption of sons." Galatians 4:5

REFUGE, *Our:* "The Lord also will be a refuge for the oppressed, a refuge in times of trouble." Psalm 9:9

"The LORD of hosts is with us; the God of Jacob is our refuge. Se-lah." Psalm 46:7

"Trust in him at all times; ye people, pour out your heart before him: God is a refuge for us." Psalm 62:8

RENEWER, *Our:* "But they that wait upon the Lord shall renew their strength; they shall mount up with wings as eagles; they shall run, and not be weary and they shall walk, and not faint." Isaiah 40:31

"Therefore if any man be in Christ, he is a new creature: old things are passed away; behold, all things are become new." 2 Corinthians 5:17

"And be renewed in the spirit of your mind; And that ye put on the new man, which after God is created in righteousness and true holiness." Ephesians 4:23-24

REST, *Our*: "And it shall come to pass in the day that the LORD shall give thee rest from thy sorrow, and from thy fear, and from the hard bondage wherein thou wast made to serve." Isaiah 14:3

"My people hath been lost sheep: their shepherds have caused them to go astray, they have turned them away on the mountains: they have gone from mountain to hill, they have forgotten their restingplace." Jeremiah 50:6

"Come unto me, all ye that labour and are heavy laden, and I will give you rest." Matthew 11:28

"Let not your heart be troubled: ye believe in God, believe also in me." John 14:1

Plug in

Lord, we've come to realize there is no rest in people,
places, or things, position, power, nor fame.
Thank you for reminding us through your Word,
we don't have to live a disturbed, restless, or anxious life.
We don't have to wonder about tomorrow nor
worry about what we will eat, drink or wear;
We don't need to worry how we're going to do this or that.
Help us to believe you have taken all our concerns on yourself,
and given us rest.

Father God, we thank and praise you for being our Resting-place.
We thank you for giving us rest from sorrow, fear,
and the bondage of sin. We thank you for making rest available
to everyone that are heavy burdened.
You've invited us to come.
Help us to accept your loving invitation
and get some rest today.

Resting in God keeps me from stressing in anything.
God, our Resting Place, we say, "thank you."

RESURRECTOR/RESURRECTION, *The:* "And they shall scourge him, and put him to death: and the third day he shall rise again." Luke 18:33

"Saying, the Lord is risen indeed, and hath appeared to Simon." Luke 24:34

"Jesus said unto her, I am the resurrection, and the life: he that believeth in me though he were dead, yet shall he live." John 11:25

"And God hath both raised up the Lord, and will also raise up us by His own power." 1 Corinthians 6:14

REVEALER, *Our:* "He revealeth the deep and secret things, he knoweth what is in darkness, and the light dwelleth with him." Daniel 2:22

"The king answered unto Daniel, and said, Of a truth it is, that your God is a God of gods, and a Lord of kings and a revealer of secrets, seeing thou couldest reveal this secret." Daniel 2:47

"For I neither received it of man, neither was I taught it, but by the revelation of Jesus Christ." Galatians 1:12

"How that by revelation he made known unto me the mystery; (as I wrote afore in few words, Whereby, when ye read, ye may understand my knowledge in the mystery of Christ)" Ephesians 3:3-4

REWARDER, *Our:* "After these things the word of the LORD came unto Abram in a vision, saying Fear not, Abram: I am thy shield, and thy exceeding great reward." Genesis 15:1

"So that a man shall say, Verily there is a reward for the righteous: verily he is a God that judgeth in the earth." Psalm 58:11

"Rejoice, and be exceeding glad: for great is your reward in heaven: for so persecuted they the prophets which were before you." Matthew 5:12

"For we must all appear before the judgment seat of Christ; that every one may receive the things done in his body, according to that he hath done, whether it be good or bad." 2 Corinthians 5:10

"But without faith it is impossible to please him, for he that cometh to God must believe that he is, and that he is a rewarder of them that diligently seek him. Hebrews 11:6

"And, behold, I come quickly; and my reward is with me, to give every man according as his work shall be." Revelation 22:12

Plug in

Let face it, who doesn't want to get paid for working in
some way, some day?
Even God in His infinite wisdom chose to offer us a pay day.
He is so wise, gracious, and kind,
He wants to wonderfully reward us every time
for the work we've done in Him.

However, God doesn't pay like man.
Everyone will get paid according to that he has done,
whether good or bad.
We can thank God whatever
He pays is the right wage.
He rewards willing workers in righteousness
and diligence in seeking Him.
He rewards the sacrifice in doing unto others
as we want done to us.
So let us thank the Lord;
He will pay every man according to his work.

God hired me a long time ago, and I'm still on His payroll.
God, our Rewarder, we say, "thank you."

RIGHTEOUS: "Hear me when I call, O God of my righteousness: thou hast enlarged me when I was in distress; have mercy upon me, and hear my prayer." Psalm 4:1

"For the righteous LORD loveth righteousness; his countenance doth behold the upright." Psalm 11:7

"To show that the LORD is upright: he is my rock, and there is no unrighteousness in him." Psalm 92:15

"The LORD is righteous in all his ways, and holy in all his works." Psalm 145:17

"In his days Judah shall be saved, and Israel shall dwell safely: and this is his name whereby he shall be called, THE LORD OUR RIGHTEOUSNESS." Jeremiah 23:6

Plug in

God is right. God is upright. God is righteous.
God is righteousness. God is just right.
That's it. That's all. God is all right.
and He's always right on time.

Lord, we offer thanksgiving and praises to you.
You are The Lord our Righteousness.
You're righteous in your thought,
righteous in your way; righteous at night,
and righteous all day.

God always has "the right of way"; any turn with Him is right.
God our Righteousness, we say, "Thank you".

ROCK, *Our:* "He is the Rock, his work is perfect: for all his ways are judgment: a God of truth and without iniquity, just and right is he." Deuteronomy 32:4

"The LORD is my rock, and my fortress, and my deliverer; my God, my strength, in whom I will trust; my buckler, and the horn of my salvation, and my high tower." Psalm 18:2

"Be thou my strong habitation, whereunto I may continually resort: thou hast given commandment to save me, for thou art my rock and my fortress." Psalm 71:3

"And did all drink the same spiritual drink: for they drank of that spiritual Rock that followed them: and that Rock was Christ." 1 Corinthians 10:4

RULER, *Our:* "For the kingdom is the LORD's: and he is the governor among the nations." Psalm 22:28

"He ruleth by his power for ever; his eyes behold the nations: let not the rebellious exalt themselves, Selah" Psalm 66:7

"Thou rulest the raging of the sea: when the waves thereof arise, thou stillest them." Psalm 89:9

S

SAFETY, *Our:* "I will both lay me down in peace, and sleep: for thou, LORD, only makest me dwell in safety." Psalm 4:8

"For the oppression of the poor, for the sighing of the needy, now will I arise saith the LORD; I will set him in safety from him that puffeth at him." Psalms 12:5

"The name of the LORD is a strong tower: the righteous runneth into it, and is safe." Proverbs 18:10

"The horse is prepared against the day of battle: but safety is of the LORD." Proverbs 21:31

SANCTIFIER, *Our:* "And ye shall keep my statutes, and do them: I am the LORD which sanctify you." Leviticus 20:8

"Unto the church of God which is at Corinth, to them that are sanctified in Christ Jesus, called to be saints, with all that in every place call upon the name of Jesus Christ our Lord, both theirs and ours:" 1 Corinthians 1:2

"Wherefore Jesus also, that he might sanctify the people with his own blood, suffered without the gate." Hebrews 13:12

"Jude, the servant of Jesus Christ, and brother of James, to them that are sanctified by God the Father, and preserved in Jesus Christ, and called:" Jude 1:1

SATISFIER, *Our:* "O satisfy us early with thy mercy; that we may rejoice and be glad all our days." Psalm 90:14

"Who satisfieth thy mouth with good things; so that thy youth is renewed like the eagle's." Psalm 103:5

"Thou openest thine hand, and satisfiest the desire of every living thing." Psalm 145:16

Plug in

Have you heard the song
"I Can't Get No Satisfaction?"
This song could very well be true,
depending on who we're looking to.
If we're looking to sin, Satan, and the world,
certainly there'll be no satisfaction here or
in the great bye and bye.
If we're looking to God, who opens His hand to
satisfy us early with His mercy;
and satisfies the desire of every living thing,
we can be assured there is complete satisfaction in Him.

Apart from God, there is nothing that satisfies.
There is nothing in man; who man is; what man has done;
what man is doing; nor in what he would aspire to do.
There is no satisfaction found in him, me, or you.
We can thank and praise God because
only He can satisfy the longing soul.

Without God, I can't get no satisfaction.
God, our Satisfier, we say, "thank you."

158

SAVIOR, *The:* "Look unto me, and be ye saved, all the ends of the earth: for I am God, and there is none else." Isaiah 45:22

"For unto you is born this day in the city of David, a Saviour, which is Christ the Lord." Luke 2:11

"And said unto the woman, Now we believe, not because of thy saying: for we have heard him ourselves, and know that this is indeed the Christ, the Saviour of the world." John 4:42

"Praising God, and having favor with all the people. And the Lord added to the church daily such as should be saved." Acts 2:47

"Neither is there salvation in any other: for there is none other name under heaven given among men, whereby we must be saved." Acts 4:12

SEALER, *Our:* "In whom ye also trusted, after that ye heard the word of truth, the gospel of your salvation: in whom also after that ye believed, ye were sealed with that holy Spirit of promise," Ephesians 1:13

"And grieve not the holy Spirit of God, whereby ye are sealed unto the day of redemption." Ephesians 4:30

"Who hath also sealed us, and given the earnest of the Spirit in our hearts." 2 Corinthians 1:22

SEER, *Our:* "The LORD looketh from heaven; he beholdeth all the sons of men. From the place of his habitation he looketh upon all the inhabitants of the earth." Psalm 33:13-14

"Thou hast set our iniquities before thee, our secret sins in the light of thy countenance." Psalm 90:8

"He that planted the ear, shall he not hear? He that formed the eye, shall he not see? Psalm 94:9

"The eyes of the LORD are in every place, beholding the evil and the good." Proverbs 15:3

"But thou, when thou prayest, enter into thy closet, and when thou hast shut thy door, pray to thy Father which is in secret; and thy Father which seeth in secret shall reward thee openly." Matthew 6:6

"In the day when God shall judge the secrets of men by Jesus Christ according to my gospel." Romans 2:16

Plug in

One thing I can testify of the Lord is, He sees all.
There is no need to worry about what we can't see,
what's hidden from our view, nor what's around the corner.
We have a God that sees in, out, over, under, through,
upside down, downside up, around, and behind.
Nothing is hidden from His eyesight. He sees right now.
We can thank Him, His eyes are in every place
"LOOKING"
at the evil and the good.
We don't have to fear; God is near.
Let's stop trying to see what we can't see.
Trust the Seer, and let it be.

**God has helped me to see, He's the Seer; not me. I can trust His
eyesight. He sees beyond 20/20.**
God, our Seer, we say, "thank you."

SHEPHERD, *The:* "The LORD is my shepherd; I shall not want." Psalm 23:1

"I am the good shepherd: the good shepherd giveth his life for the sheep." John 10:11

"And when the chief Shepherd shall appear, ye shall receive a crown of glory that fadeth not away." 1 Peter 5:4

"For ye were as sheep going astray; but are now returned unto the Shepherd and Bishop of your souls." 1 Peter 2:25

Plug in

Have you ever grammatically considered
or looked at the word 'shepherd'?
Looking closely, you may see SHEEP-HERD.
Yes, God is our Shepherd; He herds the sheep.
He's the keeper, feeder, leader, protector,
and guider of His sheep.

Father God, we thank you for being our Shepherd,
the Good Shepherd, Chief Shepherd, and Bishop of our souls.
You are our Shepherd in Word, Spirit, and action.
Thank you for leading us to the green pastures,
making us to lie down when needed.
Thank you for leading us beside still waters and
refreshing our soul; and leading us
in the way of righteousness for your name's sake.

God has shepherded me to a safe place in Him.
God, our Shepherd, we say, "thank you."

SINLESS: "He is the Rock, his work is perfect: for all his ways are judgment: a God of truth and without iniquity, just and right is he." Deuteronomy 32:4

"For he hath made him to be sin for us, who knew no sin; that we might be made the righteousness of God in him." 2 Corinthians 5:21

"For we have not an high priest which cannot be touched with the feeling of our infirmities; but was in all points tempted like as we are, yet without sin." Hebrews 4:15

"So Christ was once offered to bear the sins of many; and unto them that look for him shall he appear the second time without sin unto salvation." Hebrews 9:28

"For even hereunto were ye called: because Christ also suffered for us, leaving us an example, that ye should follow his steps: Who did no sin, neither was guile found in his mouth:" 1 Peter 2:21-22

STRENGTH, *Our:* "He is wise in heart, and mighty in strength; who hath hardened himself against him, and hath prospered?" Job 9:4

"The Lord is their strength, and he is the saving strength of his anointed." Psalm 28:8

"Thy God hath commanded thy strength: strengthen, O God, that which thou hast wrought for us." Psalm 68:28

"My flesh and my heart faileth: but God is the strength of my heart, and my portion forever." Psalm 73:26

"He giveth power to the faint; and to them that have no might he increaseth strength." Isaiah 40:29

"I can do all things through Christ which strengtheneth me.' Philippians 4:13

Plug in

Father God, we thank you for being our Strength.
You are wise in heart and mighty in strength.
You are the strength of our heart and our portion forever.
Thank you for commanding strength for us when we have no might.
Thank you for strength every day, enabling us to do all things
through Christ. When we fall, it is your strength that gets us up.
Oh Lord, we realize we are totally helpless without you.
We need your strength when we are weak.
We need your strength when feeling down and out.
We cannot make it without you; this we have no doubt.

The Lord has been my strength through Christ;
He is my Strong Arm.
God, our Strength, we say, "thank you."

165

SUPREME: "And Melchizedek king of Salem brought forth bread and wine: and he was the priest of the most high God." Genesis 14:18

"And of Zion it shall be said, This and that man was born in her: and the highest himself shall establish her." Psalm 87:5

"Thou rulest the raging of the sea: when the waves thereof arise, thou stillest them." Psalm 89:9

"The LORD is high above all nations, and his glory above the heavens." Psalm 113:4

"It is he that sitteth upon the circle of the earth, and the inhabitants thereof are as grasshoppers; that stretcheth out the heavens as a curtain, and spreadeth them out as a tent to dwell in." Isaiah 40:22

SUSTAINER, *Our:* "I laid me down and slept; I awaked; for the LORD sustained me." Psalm 3:5

"Cast thy burden upon the LORD, and he shall sustain thee: he shall never suffer the righteous to be moved." Psalm 55:22

"And he is before all things, and by him all things consist." Colossians 1:17

Plug In

I thank and praise God because He is my:

Q_____

R_____

S_____

Chapter 5

THANKING and PRAISING GOD for GOD through T, U, V

T

TEACHER, *Our:* "Good and upright is the LORD: therefore will he teach sinners in the way." Psalm 25:8

"I will instruct thee and teach thee in the way that thou shall go: I will guide thee with mine eye." Psalm 32:8

"Who hath directed the Spirit of the LORD, or being his counseller hath taught him? With whom took he counsel, and who instructed him, and taught him in the path of judgment, and taught him knowledge, and shewed to him the way of understanding?" Isaiah 40:13-14

"And Jesus went about all Galilee, teaching in their synagogues, and preaching the gospel of the kingdom, and healing all manner of sickness and all manner of disease among the people." Matthew 4:23

"And he opened his mouth, and taught them, saying." Matthew 5:2

"For the prophecy came not in old time by the will of man: but holy men of God spake as thy were moved by the Holy Ghost." 2 Peter 1:21

Plug in

Father God, we thank and praise you for being our Teacher.
Thank you for teaching us how to:

Take what you offer,
Eat what you prepare,
Accept what you did,
Come before your presence,
Help those in need,
Enter into your presence with thanksgiving; and
Run with patience the race that is set before us.

I am taught by the best: God the Father, the Son, and the Holy Spirit.
God, our Teacher, we say, "thank you."

TIME DETERMINER, *The:* "But I trusted in thee, O LORD: I said, Thou art my God. My times are in thy hand: deliver me from the hand of mine enemies, and from them that persecute me." Psalm 31:14-15

"And he changest the times and the seasons: he removeth kings, and setteth up kings: he giveth wisdom unto the wise, and knowledge to them that know understanding:" Daniel 2:21

"And hath made of one blood all nations of men for to dwell on all the face of the earth, and hath determined the times before appointed, and the bounds of their habitation;" Acts 17:26

"Humble yourselves therefore under the mighty hand of God, that he may exalt you in due time:" 1 Peter 5:6

"And the angel which I saw stand upon the sea and upon the earth lifted up his hand to heaven, and sware by him that liveth for ever and ever, who created heaven, and the things that therein are, and the earth, and the things that therein are, and the sea, and the things which are therein, that there should be time no longer." Revelation 10:5-6

TRANSGRESSION BLOTTER, *Our:* "Have mercy on me, O God, according to thy lovingkindness: according unto the multitude of thy tender mercies blot out my transgressions." Psalm 51: 1

"Hide thy face from my sins, and blot out all mine iniquities." Psalm 51:9

"Blotting out the handwriting of ordinances that was against us, which was contrary to us, and took it out of the way, nailing it to his cross;" Colossians 2:14

Plug in

When something is blotted out there is no more visualization of it.
It is gone from physical sight. It is never to be seen again.
It is erased.
That's what God did for us through Jesus Christ.
He removed our sins never to be remembered or seen again.
He did this through His precious blood.
He took our sins out of the way, nailing them to His cross.
Lord, we thank you sin is no longer blocking our way,
communion, and fellowship with you.

God has an eraser for my sin, the precious blood of Jesus.
God, our Transgression Blotter, we say, "thank you."

TRANSPORTER, *Our:* "In my Father's house are many mansions: if it were not so, I would have told you. I go to prepare a place for you. And if I go and prepare a place for you, I will come again, and receive you unto myself; that where I am, there ye may be also." John 14: 2-3

"For so an entrance shall be ministered unto you abundantly into the everlasting kingdom of our Lord and Saviour Jesus Christ." 2 Peter 1:11

TRIUMPHANT: "Then sang Moses and the children of Israel this song unto the LORD, and spake, saying, I will sing unto the LORD, for he hath triumphed gloriously: the horse and his rider hath he thrown into the sea." Exodus 15:1

"Nay, in all these things we are more than conquerors through him that loved us." Romans 8:37

"Now thanks be unto God, which always causeth us to triumph in Christ, and maketh manifest the savour of his knowledge by us in every place." 2 Corinthians 2:14

"And having soiled principalities and powers, he made a shew of them openly, triumphing over them in it." Colossians 2:15

TRUE: "But the LORD is the true God, he is the living God, and an everlasting king; at his wrath the earth shall tremble, and the nations shall not be able to abide his indignation." Jeremiah 10:10

"And we know that the Son of God is come, and hath given us an understanding, that we may know him that is true, and we are in him that is true, even in his Son Jesus Christ. This is the true God, and eternal life." 1 John 5: 20

TRUST, *Our:* "O LORD my God, in thee do I put my trust: save me from all them that persecute me, and deliver me:" Psalm 7:1

"And they that know thy name will put their trust in thee: for thou, LORD, hast not forsaken them that seek thee." Psalm 9:10

"For thou art my hope, O Lord GOD: thou art my trust from my youth." Psalm 71:5

"My goodness, and my fortress; my high tower, and my deliverer; my shield, and he in whom I trust; who subdueth my people under me." Psalm 144:2

"Trust in the LORD with all thine heart: and lean not unto thine own understanding. In all thy ways acknowledge him, and he shall direct thy paths." Proverbs 3:5-6

Plug In

Father God, we thank and praise you for being our Trust.
You have been our Trust from our youth.
You have proven to be trustworthy every step of the way.
You always do the right thing, in the right way, and at the right time.
Help us to trust you with all our heart, soul, strength, and mind.

Help us to follow your lead for you are trustworthy indeed.
We thank you for being our Trust in sickness and in health,
In good times and bad, whether in poverty or in wealth.

It pays to put all my trust in God, and not in anyone.
God, our Trust, we say, "thank you."

U

UNCHANGEABLE/UNCHANGING: "For I am the LORD, I change not; therefore ye sons of Jacob are not consumed." Malachi 3: 6

"Jesus Christ the same yesterday, and to day, and for ever." Hebrews 13:8

UNSEARCHABLE: "Hast thou not known? Hast thou not heard, that the everlasting God, the LORD, the Creator of the ends of the earth, fainteth not, neither is weary? there is no searching of his understanding." Isaiah 40:28

"O the depth of the riches both of the wisdom and knowledge of God! God how unsearchable are his judgments, and his ways past finding out! For who hath known the mind of the Lord? Or who hath been his counsellor?" Romans 11:33-34

"Unto me, who am less than the least of all saints, is this grace given, that I should preach among the Gentiles the unsearchable riches of Christ;" Ephesians 3:8

Plug in

No one can find out God;
no one knows His mind.
No one can say what God is going to do next;
how He's going to do it;
when He's going to do it;
where He's going to do it;
who He's going to do it to;
and why He's doing what He's doing.
That's why God is God.

My mind is too small to search out the unsearchable God.
God, the Unsearchable God, we say, "thank you."

UNTEMPTABLE: "Jesus said unto him, It is written again, Thou shalt not tempt the Lord thy God." Matthew 4:7

"Let no man say when he is tempted, I am tempted of God; for God; cannot be tempted with evil, neither tempteth he any man." James 1:13

UPHOLDER, *Our:* "Hold up my goings in thy paths, that my footsteps slip not." Psalm 17:5

"For the arms of the wicked shall be broken: but the LORD upholdeth the righteous." Psalm 37:17

"Though he fall, he shall not be utterly cast down: for the LORD upholdeth him with his hand." Psalm 37:24

"Hold thou me up, and I shall be safe: and I will have respect unto thy statutes continually." Psalm 119:117

"The LORD upholdeth all that fall, and raiseth up all those that be bowed down." Psalms 145:14

Plug in

Thank you Lord, for holding us up.
Without you we will surely fall.
Thank you for keeping your loving arms around us,
never letting us go.
Thank you for holding us up in the inner man.
Though our physical man may fall, we are thankful
you are able to raise all who call.

When I felt like laying down and giving up, God held me up.
God, our Upholder, we say, "thank you."

VALOR, *Our***:** "For thou hast girded me with strength unto the battle; thou hast subdued under me those that rose up against me." Psalm 18:39

"Through thee will we push down our enemies: through thy name will we tread them under that rise up against us. For I will not trust in my bow, neither shall my sword save me. But thou hast saved us from our enemies, and hast put them to shame that hated us. In God we boast all the day long, and praise thy name for ever. Se-lah." Psalm 44:5-8

"(For the weapons of our warfare are not carnal, but mighty through God to the pulling down of strongholds;)" 2 Corinthians 10:4

VICTOR/ VICTORY, *Our:* "O SING unto the LORD a new song; for he hath done marvellous things: his right hand, and his holy arm, hath gotten him the victory." Psalm 98:1

"O death, where is thy sting? O grave, where is thy victory? The sting of death is sin; and the strength of sin is the law. But thanks be to God, which giveth us the victory through our Lord Jesus Christ." 1 Corinthians 15: 55-57

Plug in

Thanks be to God,
He has won the victory through Jesus our Lord!
Victory over Satan. Victory over the world.
Victory for every little boy and girl.
Victory over death. Victory over flesh.
God gave the victory; through Him we can rest.
Victory over the grave. Victory over sin.
Because of His great love, the Victor did win!

God is the winner, and I am a recipient of His winning
through Jesus Christ our Lord.
God, our Victor, we say, "thank you."

181

Plug In

I thank and praise God because He is my:

T_____

U_____

V_____

Chapter 6

THANKING and PRAISING GOD for GOD through W, X

W

WATER OF LIFE, *The:* "Jesus answered and said unto her, If thou knewest the gift of God, and who it is that saith to thee, Give me to drink; thou wouldest have asked of him, and he would have given thee living water." John 4:10

"But whosoever drinketh of the water that I shall give him shall never thirst; but the water that I shall give him shall be in him a well of water springing up into everlasting life." John 4:14

"And the Spirit and the bride say, Come. And him that heareth say, Come. And let him that is athirst come. And whosoever will, let him take the water of life freely." Revelation 22:17

WASHER FROM INIQUITY, *Our:* "Wash me throughly from mine iniquity and cleanse me from my sin." Psalm 51:2

"Purge me with hyssop, and I shall be clean: wash me, and I shall be whiter than snow." Psalm 51:7

"And from Jesus Christ, who is the faithful witness, and the first begotten of the dead, and the prince of the kings of the earth. Unto him that loved us, and washed us from our sins in his own blood," Revelation 1:5

Plug in

Father God, we thank and adore you because you are God,
the One who washed us from our iniquity,
and cleaned us from our sin.
Thank you for purging us.
Thank you for washing us that we become whiter than snow.
Father, we thank you for not using man made bleaches,
washing powers, stain removers, or quick scrubs.
Thank you for knowing that man-made detergents
or products weren't sufficient to clean us up.
They couldn't make us pure enough to stand in your sight.
We thank and give you praise, only through the shed blood of Jesus,
(The Faithful witness, the first begotten of the dead,
and the prince of the kings of the earth),
we are washed and made clean.

God washed me, and bleached all my dirty laundry in His blood.
God, our Washer, we say, "thank you."

WAY, *The*: "Jesus saith unto him, I am the way, the truth, and the life: no man cometh unto the Father, but by me." John 14:6

"Having therefore, brethren, boldness to enter into the holiest by the blood of Jesus, By a new and living way, which he hath consecreated for us, through the veil, that is to say, his flesh;" Hebrews 10:19-20

WHICH WAS, AND IS, AND IS TO COME: "John to the seven churches which are in Asia: Grace be unto you, and peace, from him which is, and which was, and which is to come; and from the seven Spirits which are before his throne;" Revelation 1:4

"I am the Alpha and the Omega, the beginning and the ending," saith the Lord, "which is, and which was, and which is to come, the Almighty." Revelation 1:8

WORD, *The*: "In God will I praise his word: in the LORD will I praise his word." Psalm 56:10

"In the beginning was the Word, and the Word was with God, and the Word was God." John 1:1

"And the Word was made flesh, and dwelt among us, (and we beheld his glory, the glory as of the only begotten of the Father,) full of grace and truth." John 1:14

"And being found in fashion as a man, he humbled himself, and became obedient unto death, even the death of the cross." Philippians 2:8

"That which was from the beginning, which we have heard, which we have seen with our eyes, which we have looked upon, and our hands have handled, of the Word of life;" 1 John 1:1

Plug in

Father God, we thank and give you praise for your Word.
Your Word was made flesh, and came and lived among us:
The Word, The Living Word, The Word for the world;
The Word in the world, The Word of:
Wisdom, Origin of life, Redemption, Deliverance.

What mercy! What love! What grace and truth!
The Word, our lamp; the Word, our light;
the Word in the beginning;
the Word we've heard; the Word we've seen; the Word that was;
the Word that is; the Word to come; the Word we praise;
the Word we've handled, of the Word of life.
That living Word is Christ.

I've discovered, God is not in hiding;
I can always find Him in His Word.
God, the Word, we say, "thank you."

WORKER, *Our:* "Jesus answered, Neither hath this man sinned, nor his parents; but that the works of God should be made manifest in him. I must work the works of him that sent me, while it is day: the night cometh, when no man can work." John 9:3-4

"In whom also we have obtained an inheritance, being predestinated according to the purpose of him who worketh all things after the counsel of his own will:" Ephesians 1:11

"Whereunto I also labour, striving according to his working, which worketh in me mightily." Colossians 1:29.

Plug in

Oh Father, we thank you for being our Worker.
There is no work like your work.
Thank you for working in us mightily.
Thank you for working in and on our heart to know you better.
Thank you that we may know the job you have assigned us to.
Whatever it takes Lord, work in us.
If you need a hammer to pound out the sin from our heart;
work it out, Lord, work.
If you need a drill to power out bitterness;
work it out, Lord, work.
If you need nails to fasten out proudness;
work it out, Lord, work.
Whatever tool it takes, please Lord use it
to work in us mightily to your glory and praise.

Work in us the love of God, and the love for others.
Work in us the peace and righteousness of God.
Oh God, work in us to do your will;
night is coming and no man will be able to work.
Help us to work while it is day.

God never works in me haphazardly; He has a well-planned plan.
God, our Worker, we say, "thank you."

WORSHIP, *Our*: "But as for me, I will come into thy house in the multitude of thy mercy: and in thy fear will I worship toward thy holy temple." Psalm 5:7

"All nations whom thou hast made shall come and worship before thee, O Lord: and shall glorify thy name." Psalm 86:9

"Then saith Jesus unto him, Get thee hence, Satan: for it is written, Thou shalt worship the Lord thy God, and him only shalt thou serve." Matthew 4:10

"Saying with a loud voice, Fear God, and give glory to him; for the hour of his judgment is come: and worship him that made heaven, and earth, and the sea, and the fountains of waters." Revelation 14:7

"And I John saw these things, and heard them. And when I had heard and seen, I fell down to worship before the feet of the angel which shewed me these things. Then saith he unto me, See thou do it not: for I am thy fellowservant, and of thy brethren the prophets, and of them which keep the sayings of this book: worship God." Revelation 22:8-9

X

X-RAY OF LIFE, *The:* "If I say, Surely the darkness shall cover me; even the night shall be light about me. Yea, the darkness hideth not from thee; but the night shineth as the day: the darkness and the light are both alike to thee." Psalm 139:11-12

"For the word of God is quick, and powerful, and sharper than any twoedged sword, piercing even to the dividing asunder of soul and spirit, and of the joints and marrow, and is a discerner of the thoughts and intents of the heart. Neither is there any creature that is not manifest in his sight: but all things are naked and opened unto the eyes of him with whom we have to do." Hebrews 4:12-13

Plug in

An x-ray is used in medical evaluations to see past the outer into the inner
parts of the body. It is used to detect the slightest and
minutest discoveries,
which tend to be beyond and hidden from the naked eye.
The x-ray sees what the naked eye cannot.
We thank God, he not only sees what the naked eye cannot,
but into and through our flesh to the very motives of the heart.

His tool is sharper than any man-made instrument.
He alone can pierce between the dividing of soul and spirit,
the joints and marrow, to the intentions of the heart.
Only God is the X-ray of our life. He sees all of it.
He detects what is going on and corrects it.
He sees all of me and you, in, out, and through.
God's x-ray tool is His Word. His Word cuts, divides,
and pierces what is wrong on the inside.
Lord, thank you for seeing into our very core
to that which needs to become more like you.

God has always seen right through me, and still does.
God, the X-ray of Life, we say, "thank you."

Plug In

I thank and praise God because He is my:

W_____

X_____

Chapter 7

THANKING and PRAISING GOD for GOD through Y & Z

Y

YOKE RELEASER, *Our:* "And it shall come to pass in that day, that his burden shall be taken away from off thy shoulder, and his yoke from off thy neck, and the yoke shall be destroyed because of the anointing." Isaiah 10:27

"Is not this the fast that I have chosen? to loose the bands of wickedness, to undo the heavy burdens, and to let the oppressed go free, and that ye break every yoke?" Isaiah 58:6

"For now will I break his yoke from off thee, and will burst thy bonds in sunder." Nahum 1:13

"Take my yoke upon you and learn of me: for I am meek and lowly in heart: and ye shall find rest for your souls. For my yoke is easy, and my burden is light." Matthew 11:29-30

"Stand fast therefore in the liberty wherewith Christ hath made us free, and be not entangled again with the yoke of bondage." Galatians 5:1

Plug in

Have you been in a situation
where you felt you could never rise;
that this really was it?
Where the pressures of life became so burdensome
you felt suppressed and tied down?
If you are like many of us, you may have.
The good news, you don't have to stay that way.
We have help.
There is someone who is able to remove the yoke off our shoulder.
That someone is God through Jesus Christ our Lord.
He is able to release us of any burden we may be trying
to pull or carry.
I implore you to give Him that burden. Then and only then can
we take His yoke
upon us and find rest for our souls.
Let us thank God through Christ, our release has come!

I can declare, no more bondage; I have been
released by the Blood!
God, our Yoke Releaser, we say, "thank you."

Z

ZEST FOR LIVING, *Our:* "Thou hast put gladness in my heart, more than in the time that their corn and their wine increased." Psalm 4:7

"Be glad in the LORD, and rejoice, ye righteous: and shout for joy, all ye that are upright in heart." Psalm 32:11

"Make a joyful noise unto the LORD, all ye lands. Serve the LORD with gladness: come before his presence with singing." Psalms 100:1-2

"This is the day which the LORD hath made; we will rejoice and be glad in it." Psalm 118:24

"And he leaping up stood, and walked, and entered with them into the temple, walking, and leaping, and praising God." Acts 3:8

"For in him we live, and move, and have our being; as certain also of your own poets have said, For we are also his offspring." Acts 17: 28

"Not slothful in business; fervent in spirit; serving the Lord;" Romans 12:11

"But it is good to be zealously affected always in a good thing, and not only when I am present with you." Galatians 4:18

"Who gave himself for us, that he might redeem us from all iniquity, and purify unto himself a peculiar people, zealous of good works." Titus 2:14

"*Plug in*"

Do you have a zest for God?
Has He become your motivation for living?
Is He your delight?
Do you consider it's a thrill to be in His presence?
Do you wake filled with gratitude
for the privilege to commune with the One who is Holy?
As sinful and wretched as we are, He still beckons us to come
and kneel down before Him. God still wants us.
He loves us.
Let's be thankful for another opportunity to zestfully
live for our Lord.
Let us show the world we serve a risen Savior
that is very much alive today! No matter what we're going through,
we can always lift our hands in grateful praise to Him.
We can lift our head and leap for joy to see another day!
Now let's walk with vigor, vitality, and enthusiasm
by the way we live, move, and exist in Him.

God recharges my battery every time,
by renewing my spirit every day!
God, our Zest for Living, we say, "thank you."

196

Plug In

I thank and praise God because He is my:

y_____

z_____

From this day forward

From this day forward, let's begin thanking and praising God for God from A to Z. In this you will see we all have something to be thankful for no matter how bad things seem to be. We can thank God bad in any situation isn't what bad could really have been. No matter how down and depressed we may have felt, we can be thankful we got through it. During times like these, I encourage you to hold on to what you know about God according to His Word. Thank Him for being the Good, Lifter, and your Hope in those situations.

Yes, I'm deeply aware we sometime struggle with expressing gratitude when negative or bad situations pop up in our lives. For instance, I doubt we would immediately think to be thankful for our car stopping on the freeway in the 4 o'clock traffic in 105degree temperature? No—of course not. But I encourage you from this day forward, to acknowledge God by using His Word on that situation. Thank Him for being your Protector, Keeper, and Safety. Could God possibly want to give you a new car so you could *safely* travel and serve Him better?

Rest assured, if we look spiritually hard and deep enough into God's Word, we can see the good resulting from every tragedy, whether it affects directly or worldwide. We must be prayerful and grateful enough to know we're coming out, or God has something He wants to bring out of us. Let's practice using His Word in every walk of life (not only to thank Him for His provisions) but to thank Him for Him, our Source, who knows all, hears all, and sees all.

From this day forward, you will see yourself rise up, over, and beyond any obstacle that tries to block or stop your heart's gratitude toward Him. God said in His Word, He'll give us, "...the oil of joy for mourning, the garment of praise for the spirit of heaviness..." (Isaiah 61:3). In this scripture we can see God as our "Swapper". Let's thank Him that He wants to swap our bad time for His good time, our mourning for His joy, and our heaviness for His praise. Let's swap with our Lord today. What I've shared with you through Scripture, I beg you to swap.

Lastly, from this day forward, let's express our deep gratitude to God for God: "That the God of our Lord Jesus Christ, the Father of glory, may give unto you the spirit of wisdom and revelation in the knowledge of him: The eyes of your understanding be enlightened; that ye may know what is the hope of his calling, and what riches of the glory of his inheritance in the saints, And what is the exceeding greatness of his power to us-ward who believe, according to the working of his mighty power," (Ephesians 1:17-19). "Giving thanks unto the Father, which hath made us meet to be partakers of the inheritance of the saints in light: Who hath delivered us from the power of darkness, and hath translated us into the kingdom of his dear Son:" (Colossians 1:12-13).

Praying our Spiritual ABC's

- Father God, we thank You, our:

All in All, Bringer, Calmer, Deliverer, Energizer, Filler, Goer, Helper, Igniter, Justifier, Keeper, Lifter, Manager, Navigator, Overcomer, Provider, Quieter, Restorer, Savior, Teacher, Unifier, Vindicator, Willing Sacrifice, X-ray of Life, Yoke Releaser, and Zapper

- Father God, we thank You for:

All You've done for us:
Bringing us out of darkness;
Calming our spirit;
Delivering us from evil;
Energizing us to do what we need to do;
Filling us with Your Spirit;
Going all the way to Calvary;

Helping us today;
Igniting our hearts with Your love;
Justifying us through Your blood;
Keeping us every day;

Lifting our heads;
Managing our moves;
Navigating our steps;
Overcoming the devil;
Providing the gift of salvation;

Quieting our spirit;
Restoring us;
Saving us;

Teaching us;
Unifying our life in Christ;
Vindicating us from sin;

Willing to die and get up again;
X-raying our every move;

Yoking up with You; and
Zapping out the enemy's blows.

About the Author

*H*ertistine resides in Los Angeles, California. She is the sixth oldest of twelve siblings. She serves and volunteers in several ministries in her local church, and finds great pleasure in helping and encouraging others to be thankful in everything. Her motto is, "Keep on Thanking." Her writing reflects her love and gratitude to God for God and others, Scripture, life experiences, prayer and praise, with a twist of poetry.

Born and raised in a small town in the open Mississippi Delta, Hertistine has come to love and appreciate God, the head of her life. She understands He is the One responsible for her being. She was brought up and taught to love and respect God. As a child one of the highlights of her life, at the end of a work week, was to go to church. She enjoyed going to church and learning about God. She grew up in a church that was not only a place she had fun in socializing with neighbors from miles and miles around, but a place to come together and worship God in spirit and in truth.

Hertistine is a wife of 40 years, mother of 4, grandmother of 3, and a retired preschool teacher. She is a graduate of California State University Dominguez Hills, with a Bachelor of Arts degree in Human Services. While struggling with finding a major in college, she knew she wanted to major in something that would help her be a help to someone else. Her love for children and people inspired *her to major in a field of study that would engage the participants in a hands-on learning capacity. She found this fulfillment and joy in working with preschool children. While working in this profession, she experienced one of life's most rewarding lesson; the lesson of being thankful from the smallest perspective in her life.*

Although she enjoys writing, gardening, thrift shopping, decorating, snapping pictures, and spending precious moments with family and friends, it was her love for teaching preschool children that provided the foundational structure for writing this book. Thankful for being given a passion for teaching children the fundamentals of learning (inclusive of their ABC's), has caused her to realize there are basic, yet profound elements of gratitude she can only ascribe to God. Using that foundational structure on a higher level of learning, has motivated her to share what she has come to know about God. Her hope and prayer, to God is that everyone who reads this book will experience a deeper, yet higher level of thankfulness to the God of our Salvation. Pulling from the structure of teaching younger children their ABC's, she happily and gratefully shares we have Something to Thank About from A to Z.

To Claudia,

Many Blessings,

Herbert Mosgan

9/22/18

CPSIA information can be obtained
at www.ICGtesting.com
Printed in the USA
FSOW01n1112041216
27974FS